Letts

Revision Notes

GCSE SUCCESS

Geography

Author
Adam Arnell

Series editor
Alan Brewerton

First published 1998
Reprinted 1998, 1999
This edition 1999

Letts Educational, 9–15 Aldine Street, London W12 8AW
Tel. 0208 740 2270
Fax 0208 740 2280

Editorial, design and production by Hart McLeod, Cambridge

British Library Cataloguing-in-Publication Data
A CIP record for this book is available from the British Library

ISBN 1 84085 298 4

Printed and bound in Italy

Letts Educational is the trading name of BPP (Letts Educational) Ltd

Contents

Physical Geography

Human Geography

Environmental Geography

Introduction

This book has been specifically designed to help you prepare for your GCSE exams in the easiest and most effective way. Keep this book with you throughout your revision – it is the key to your success.

How to use this book

All the information you need to know for your course is presented as a series of brief facts and explanations. These will help you understand and remember your work. You can work through the book chapter by chapter or you can find individual topics by using the index at the back of the book. The example below shows how pages are organised to help you revise each topic.

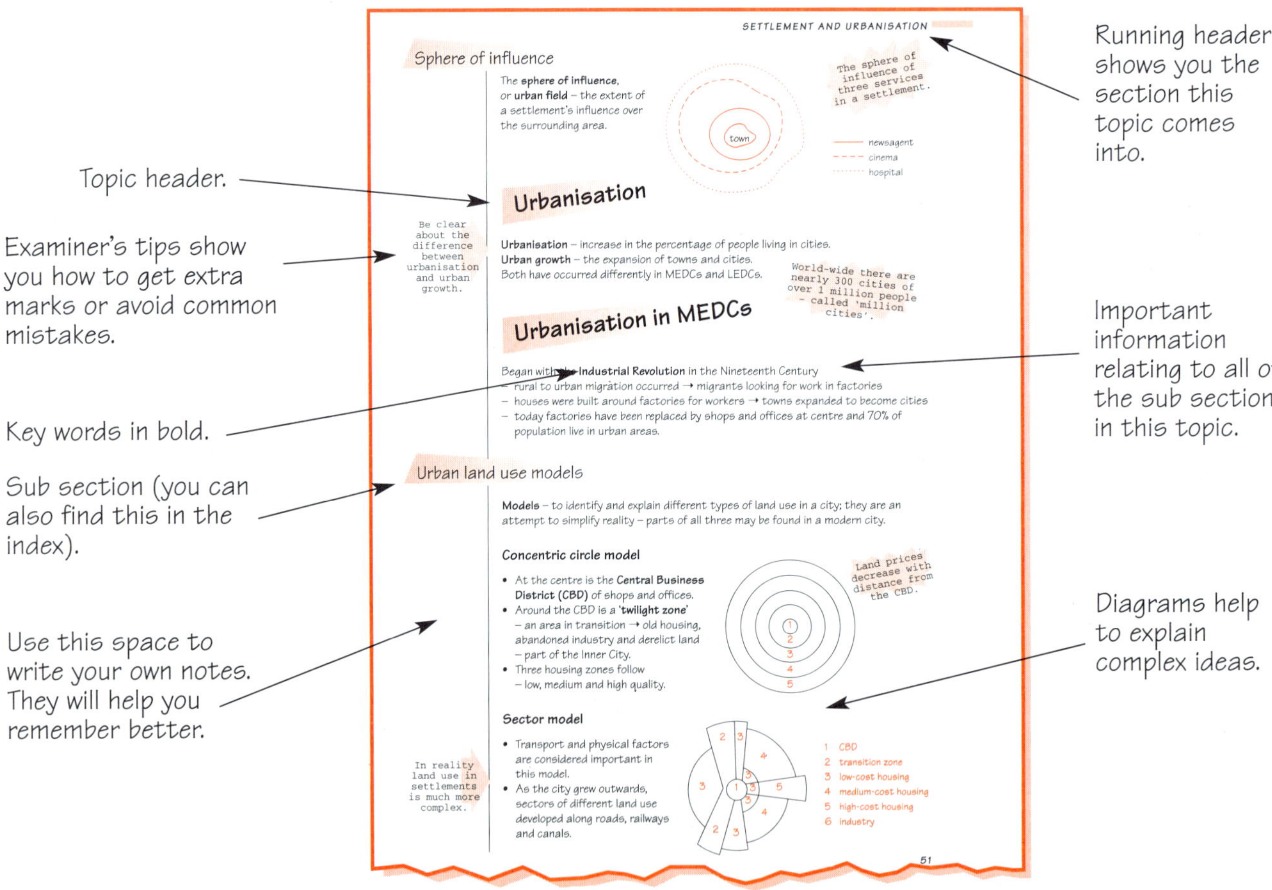

SETTLEMENT AND URBANISATION

Sphere of influence

The **sphere of influence**, or **urban field** – the extent of a settlement's influence over the surrounding area.

The sphere of influence of three services in a settlement.

town

newsagent

cinema

hospital

Urbanisation

Be clear about the difference between urbanisation and urban growth.

Urbanisation – increase in the percentage of people living in cities.

Urban growth – the expansion of towns and cities.

Both have occurred differently in MEDCs and LEDCs.

World-wide there are nearly 300 cities of over 1 million people – called 'million cities'.

Urbanisation in MEDCs

Began with the **Industrial Revolution** in the Nineteenth Century

– rural to urban migration occurred → migrants looking for work in factories

– houses were built around factories for workers → towns expanded to become cities

– today factories have been replaced by shops and offices at centre and 70% of population live in urban areas.

Urban land use models

Models – to identify and explain different types of land use in a city; they are an attempt to simplify reality – parts of all three may be found in a modern city.

Concentric circle model

- At the centre is the **Central Business District (CBD)** of shops and offices.
- Around the CBD is a **'twilight zone'** – an area in transition → old housing, abandoned industry and derelict land – part of the Inner City.
- Three housing zones follow – low, medium and high quality.

Land prices decrease with distance from the CBD.

Sector model

- Transport and physical factors are considered important in this model.
- As the city grew outwards, sectors of different land use developed along roads, railways and canals.

In reality land use in settlements is much more complex.

1 CBD

2 transition zone

3 low-cost housing

4 medium-cost housing

5 high-cost housing

6 industry

51

Preparing your revision programme

In most subjects you will have coursework, homework, revision, practice examination questions and a final examination. The examination may cause you the most anxiety. With proper preparation, however, you do not need to worry. Remember that there is a short test at the end of each topic. This test will help your understanding and boost your memory. Make sure that you have allowed enough time to revise your work and make a list of all the things you have to do and your coursework deadlines.

Most of all: **Good luck with your revision and your examinations.**

Earthquakes and volcanoes

Tectonics is the study of the forces which shape the Earth's crust – leading to the formation of volcanoes, mountains, ocean trenches and causing earthquakes.

Structure of the Earth

Earth – the fifth largest of the nine planets which orbit the Sun – formed 4600 million years ago – spheroid in shape.

Four layers

- **Crust** – a relatively very thin layer of solid rocks around the outside of the Earth
  either
  Oceanic (**sima**) – *dense*, **mainly basalt**, – between 5 and 10 km thick *or*
  Continental (**sial**) – *less dense*, **mainly granite**, between 25 and 90 km thick.
- **Mantle** – a layer of rock 2900 km thick beneath the crust, very hot but solid due to intense pressure – moves very slowly like plasticine.
- **Outer core** – a layer of molten rock 2900 to 5000 km below the crust – possibly a nickel-iron alloy.
- **Inner core** – the centre of the Earth – possibly a solid ball of nickel and iron – radius 1400 km – temperature of about 2700°C.

The mantle is **not** liquid.

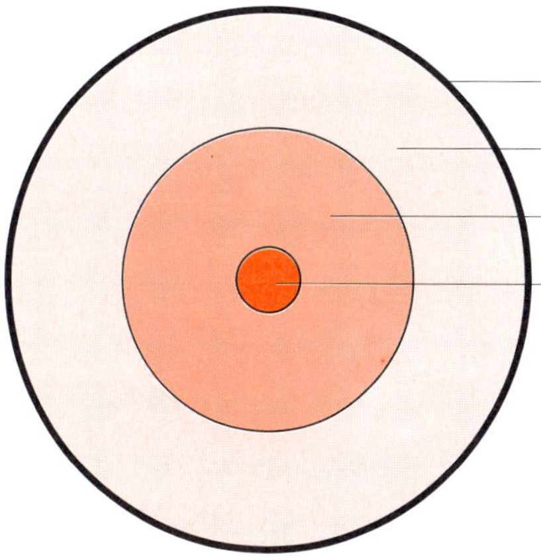

The Earth remains incredibly hot at the core; heat from when the Earth was formed, and from radioactive processes.

Plate tectonics

Plate tectonics theory developed in the 1960s
- the Earth's crust is divided into large sections called **plates** – 7 major plates, 12 smaller ones
- some plates are made of continental crust, while others are made of oceanic crust
- heat rises from the core through the mantle as **convection currents** → plates move in response
- plates move slowly – between a few millimetres and 10 cm a year – significant movement occurs over millions of years.

200 million years ago all the continents were one – known as Pangaea. Observe how closely Africa and South America would fit together.

Plate margins

Plates may move away from each other, collide or slide past each other – four plate margins or boundaries result.

Constructive margins

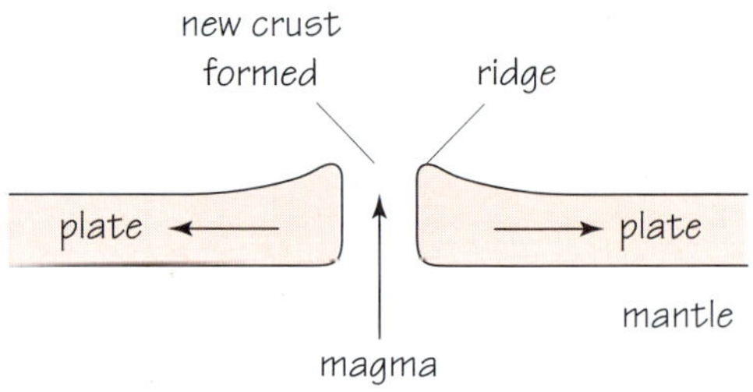

Oceanic plates **diverge**, e.g. the mid-Atlantic Ocean.

- pressure is released → rock in the mantle becomes molten (**magma**) and escapes through the gap as an eruption of **lava** → forms new crust and allows the sea floor to spread
- **mid-ocean ridge** (undersea volcanic mountain chain) develops – where volcanoes emerge above the sea, islands will form, e.g. Iceland
- minor earthquakes and volcanic eruptions occur.

Destructive margins

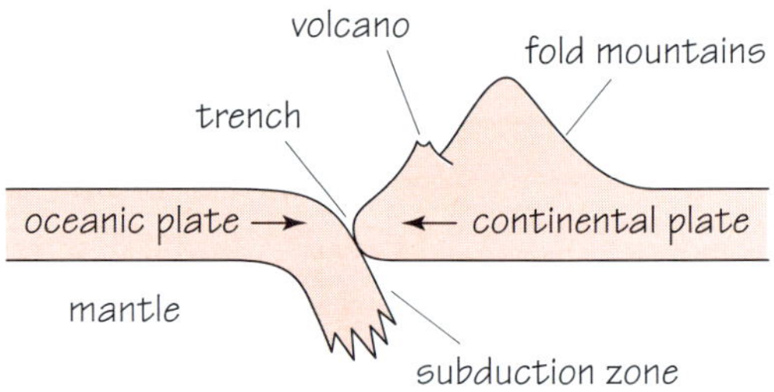

Oceanic and continental plates **converge**, e.g. Japan.

Living on plate margins has advantages and disadvantages.

- the oceanic plate, more dense than the continental plate, is forced down into the mantle – **subduction**
- deep **ocean trench** is produced – the Marianas trench (Pacific Ocean) is the deepest at over 10000 metres below sea level
- the mantle melts the oceanic plate
- forms magma → erupts as volcanoes
- the continental plate is buckled up – forms a series of **fold mountains**
- the plates move → pressure is released as shock waves → powerful earthquakes.

Collision margins

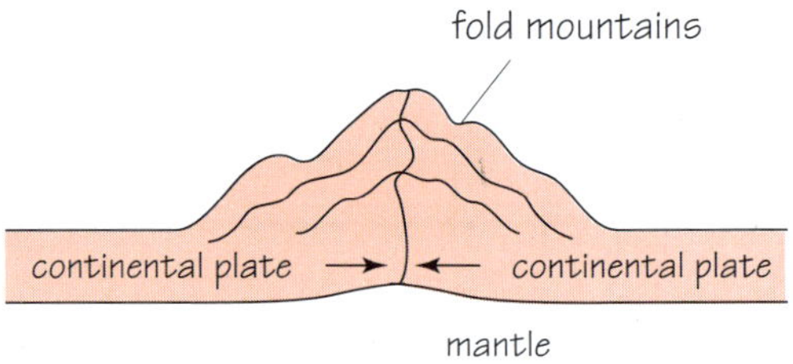

Continental plates **converge**

- neither plate dense enough to 'sink' into the mantle – both are buckled to form fold mountains, e.g. Himalayas – highest point is Mt Everest at 8850 metres
- no volcanic eruptions but violent earthquakes.

Conservative margins

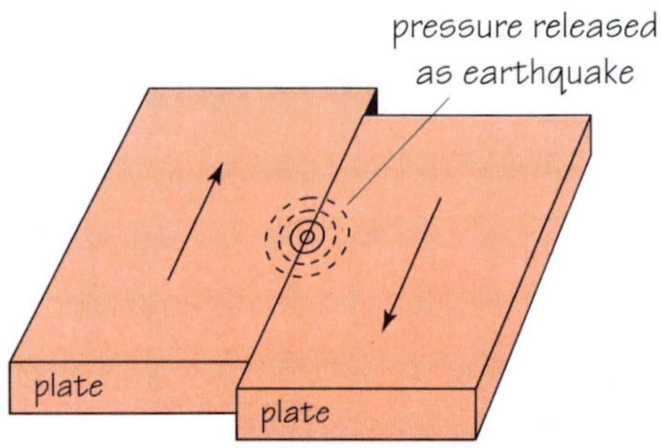

Two plates move past each other, e.g. San Andreas Fault, California

- pressure builds up – the plates finally move, energy released as a powerful earthquake
- no crust created or destroyed, no volcanic eruptions.

Two plates moving in the same direction but at different speeds are also conservative margins.

Volcanoes

Molten rock is called magma when it is underground; lava once it reaches the surface.

Volcano – an opening in the Earth's crust through which lava, ash and gas are ejected. Classified as **active** if they have erupted recently, **dormant** if they have erupted in the last 2000 years, **extinct** if they have not erupted for many thousands or millions of years.

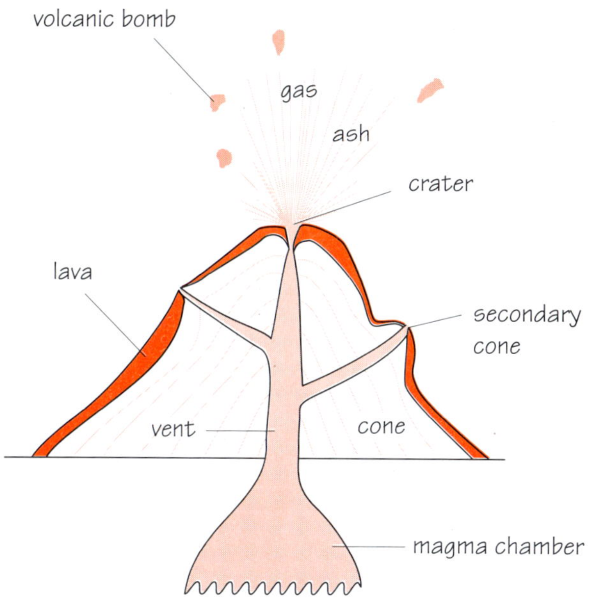

Causes

Most volcanoes occur on plate margins.

- **Destructive plate margins** – oceanic crust is melted as it is subducted – magma forces its way upwards through the continental crust to erupt as explosive volcanoes, e.g. Mt St Helens.
- **Constructive plate margins** – lava rises to fill the gap as two plates pull apart – relatively gentle eruptions, e.g. Iceland.
- **Hot spots** – chambers of magma develop in the mantle – melt through crust – long gentle eruptions of lava, e.g. Hawaii.
- **Fissure eruptions** – a weak spot, a fault, allows lava to break through – long gentle eruptions form large flat areas (**plateaus**) called **flood basalts**, e.g. Isle of Skye.

Types

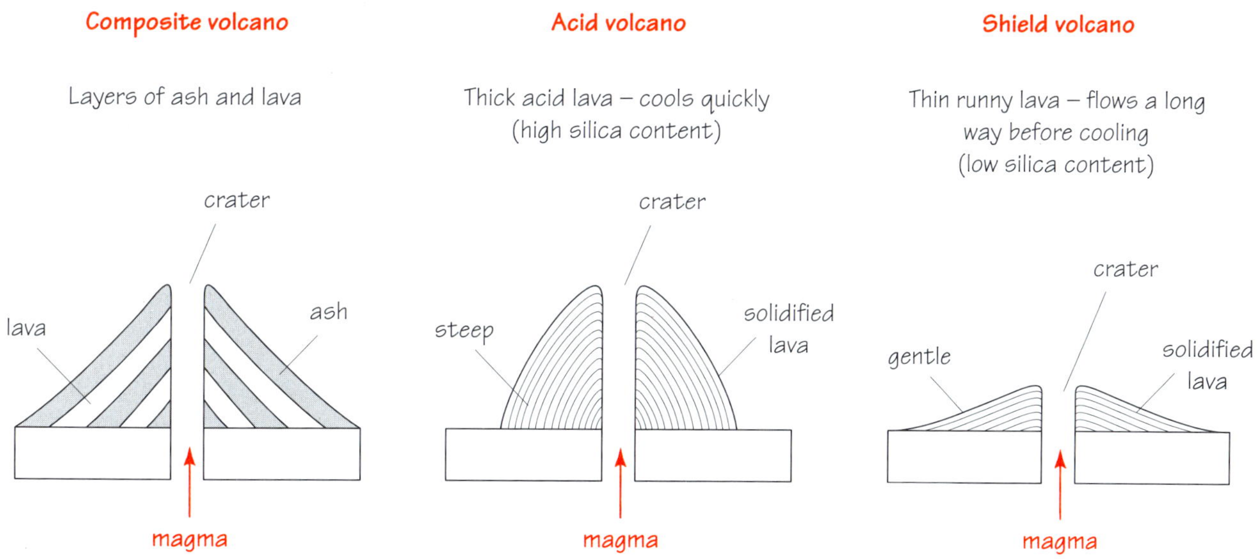

Effects of an explosive volcanic eruption

- **Pyroclastic flows** – clouds of extremely hot gas and ash (**nuées ardents**) avalanche down the side of a volcano – blast flattens and burns trees and buildings.
- **Lahars** – very fast mudflows – ash mixing with rain or melted glacier – cause massive destruction (block river valleys).
- **Lava flows** – rivers of molten rock burn and bury anything in path.
- **Ash fall** – millions of tons of ash may fall – buries buildings, roads and kills vegetation – area uninhabitable.
- **Global climate** – ash ejected from volcano is carried high into atmosphere – reflects sunlight – makes world climate cooler.

Earthquakes

Earthquake – a series of **seismic waves** (shockwaves) that travel through the Earth and around the crust.

Causes

Earthquakes may occur many miles from plate margins along fault lines in the crust.

- Occur at all plate margins – particularly severe at **destructive margins**.
- **Pressure** builds up at plate margins over many years – movement prevented by **friction** – finally the crust breaks along a **fault** – the plates move – stored energy is released in a few seconds and travels outwards as shockwaves.
- **Focus** – point at which the energy is released.
- **Epicentre** – the surface point directly above focus.

Effects

Effects of earthquakes and volcanoes are more severe in LEDCs than MEDCs; be prepared to explain why.

- buildings collapse trapping and killing people inside
- structures, e.g. bridges and elevated roads – collapse, crushing cars
- materials, e.g. signs and glass – fall from buildings injuring people below
- gas pipes are broken and gas ignited – many people may die in **firestorms**
- water pipes broken → no water to fight fires
- shortage of drinking water → disease quickly spreads
- roads buckle – emergency access restricted
- industries cannot operate → very expensive to repair damage → long term impact on economy.

- **Liquefaction** may occur – clay behaves as a liquid and buildings sink.
- **Tsunamis** – tidal waves up to 30 metres high – hit coastal areas.

Measurement

- **Seismographs** – record earthquake shockwaves.
- The **Richter Scale** measures the energy released in an earthquake – a **logarithmic** scale (each level of magnitude is ten times more powerful than the previous).
- **Mercalli Scale** – measures damage caused → a descriptive scale ranging from 1 (rarely felt) to 12 (total devastation).

Hazard Management

Despite much research it is not yet possible to predict earthquakes

- **richer countries** prepare – build **earthquake proof buildings**, e.g. buildings with flexible rubber foundations
- draw up **emergency plans** – buy **specialist equipment**, e.g. infra red cameras, used to search for survivors
- **poorer countries** suffer more fatalities – brick buildings cannot sway
- lack resources to deal with after effects – lack of medicine and hospitals – poor communications.

Benefits of living on plate margins

- **Fertile soils** – from weathered volcanic ash and lava.
- **Geothermal energy** – steam provides electricity and central heating.
- **Tourism** – visitors come to see features such as **geysers** and **bubbling mud pools**.
- **Minerals** – gold and diamonds are found in volcanic areas.

Earthquakes and volcanoes

Questions

1 What are the two types of crust?

2 Why do continental and oceanic plates move?

3 What is a constructive margin?

4 How are fold mountains formed?

5 On which type of plate margin do ocean trenches form?

6 Which plate boundaries do not have volcanoes?

7 What is a composite volcano?

8 What is a 'lahar'?

9 How can volcanoes affect the world's climate?

10 What is an 'epicentre'?

11 What is 'liquefaction'?

12 What instrument is used to record earthquakes?

13 What does the Mercalli scale measure?

14 Why do poorer countries suffer more damage in an earthquake?

15 Why are volcanic areas good for farming?

Rocks, resources and landscapes

Rocks are **weathered** and **eroded** to produce distinctive landscapes.
Rocks and their **minerals** are a **resource** which people exploit.

Rock groups

Rocks are made up of different minerals – some rocks contain many – others only one.

Three basic **groups** of rock.

- **Igneous** – formed from molten rock – magma; **Extrusive igneous** cools quickly at surface – **lava; Intrusive igneous** cools slowly underground – **batholith.**
- **Sedimentary** – formed by particles deposited in layers (**strata**) – compacted together – usually formed on sea bed.
- **Metamorphic** – rocks changed by extreme **heat** and/or **pressure** – formed from igneous and sedimentary rocks.

Rock types

Most rocks take millions of years to form.

Within the three groups are many different types.

Igneous

- **Basalt** – volcanic magma cools quickly at surface → tiny grains – dark colour.
- **Granite** – magma cools slowly underground → large crystals of different colours.

Sedimentary

- **Chalk** – formed in layers on shallow sea bed from shells of tiny sea creatures – white.
- **Limestone** – formed from coral, shells and skeletons of sea creatures – deposited in layers on sea bed – fossils – yellow to grey colour.
- **Coal** – layers of decayed vegetation – compacted by other sedimentary rocks.
- **Sandstone** – grains of sand compacted and cemented together – formed on sea bed or in deserts – many colours.
- **Clay** – silt carried by rivers deposited on sea bed – compacted – soft rock – brown/grey colour.

Metamorphic

- **Marble** – changed from chalk and limestone.
- **Slate** – changed from clay and mudstone.
- **Quartzite** – changed from sandstone – contains silica.

Rock characteristics

Be clear about the difference between porous and pervious rocks.

- **Hardness** – the strength of a rock – resistance to weathering and erosion.
- **Bedding Planes** – horizontal layers (strata) in a rock.
- **Joints** – vertical cracks in a rock formed by folding (tectonic movements), or shrinking when cooling (igneous) or drying (sedimentary).
- **Fault** – a fracture in the rock caused by movement in the Earth's crust.
- **Impermeable** – water is not able to pass through the rock.
- **Porous** – water is able to pass through, or be stored in, **pores** in the rock.
- **Pervious** – water is able to pass through **cracks** and **joints** in the rock.

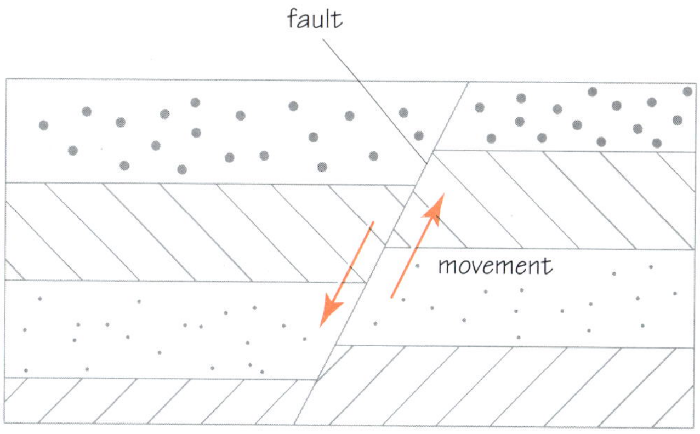

Weathering and erosion

- **Weathering** – the natural process of breaking down rocks at the Earth's surface – three types.
- **Erosion** – the process by which weathered rock is removed. Agents of erosion – **glaciers, rivers, the sea, wind**.

Physical weathering

Freeze thaw can only occur when temperature goes below, then above 0°C.

- **Freeze thaw** (frost shattering) – water seeps into crack → freezes → turns to ice → expands 9% → pressure enlarges crack → ice melts.

cold climates

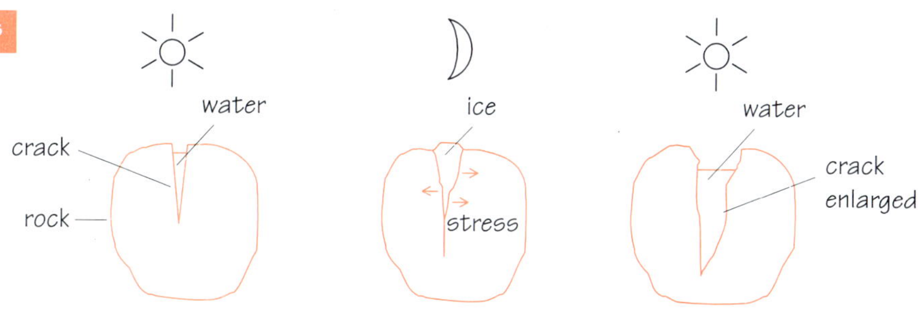

- **Exfoliation** (onion skin) – sun heats outer layer of rock → expands → at night cools → contracts → stress causes rock to crack → breaks away in layers.

hot climates

Common in deserts.

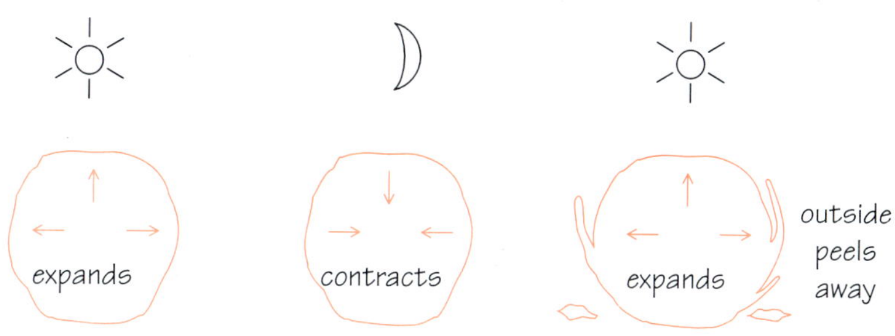

Chemical weathering

- **Warm** and **wet** climates provide most effective conditions.
- **Solution** – rainwater slightly acidic (**carbonic acid**) → dissolves **calcium carbonate** in limestone – Acid Rain (**sulphuric** and **nitric acid**) is increasing rate of process.
- **Oxidation** – oxygen dissolved in water reacts with rock minerals → minerals 'rust'.

Biological weathering

- **Trees and plants** – roots grow into cracks → exert pressure → crack enlarged.
- **Animals and insects** – burrow and tunnel – weather bedrock.

Mass movement

Mass movement – the movement of rock and soil down a slope – may occur quickly or over a long period of time.

Rapid mass movement – a **hazard** for people – both at the top and bottom of a slope.

Slopes will slowly move backwards due to mass movement.

- **Soil creep** – very slow movement of soil down a slope – caused by throughflow and run off – results in bent trees and fences → **terracettes** form.
- **Mud flow** – rapid movement of clay – rock weakened by saturation → acts as liquid.
- **Landslide** – rapid movement of rock along a curved **slip plane** (rotational slip) – caused by heavy rain or earthquake.
- **Rock fall** – a very rapid fall of cliff material (**avalanche**) loosened by weathering – fallen material (**scree**) accumulates at foot of cliff → forms **scree slopes**.

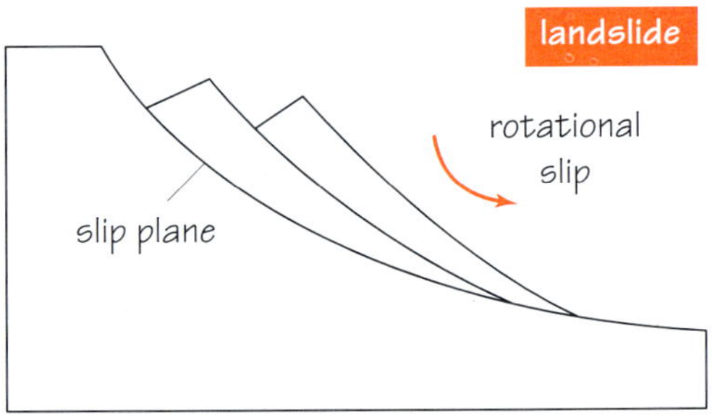

Landscapes

Granite, chalk, clay and limestone each have distinctive landscapes.

Granite

Granite – a very hard, **intrusive**, **igneous** rock, forming mountainous or moorland areas – a result of **batholiths**, **sills** and **dykes**.

There is a close relationship between rock type and land use.

- **Batholiths** – major igneous intrusions which are resistant to erosion.
- **Sills** – minor horizontal intrusions – form long ridges.
- **Dykes** – minor vertical intrusions – form long ridges or depressions.
- Impermeable → poor surface drainage → **waterlogged soil**.
- Highly **jointed** due to cooling – areas with fewer joints are more resistant to weathering → have survived as outcrops of rock known as **tors**.
- **Moors** – granite uplands – used for sheep farming and forestry – not suitable for arable farming.

Physical, chemical and biological weathering work together.

- **Recreation** – provided by granite areas → walking, and in winter possibly skiing.
- **Reservoirs** may be built in granite areas as it is strong and impermeable.

Hadrian's Wall is built along Great Whin Sill.

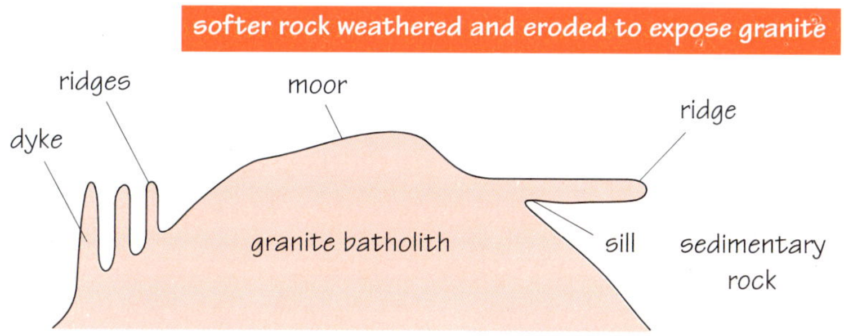

Chalk

Chalk – a relatively soft **sedimentary** rock, forming **escarpments** – a line of hills (**downs**) with a steep **scarp slope** and gentle **dip slope**.

- **Porous** → ability to absorb water resists erosion of surface.
- **Surface drainage** (rivers) – very limited.
- **Dry valleys** exist (valleys with no rivers) – possibly formed during ice age – ground frozen → behaved as impermeable rock → valleys eroded by surface streams.
- **Settlements** rare due to difficulty of obtaining water.
- **Thin soils** – with fertiliser and irrigation, arable farming is possible.
- **Water source** – water stored in chalk is called an aquifer.
- **Boreholes** used to extract water for homes and industry.

Clay

The word 'relief' means 'shape of the land'.

Clay – a very soft **sedimentary** rock forming low-lying areas with gentle **relief** – occuring in the same locations as chalk.

- **Impermeable** → many rivers flow over its surface causing gradual erosion.
- **Spring-line** villages developed at foot of downs where water came to surface.
- **Arable** and **pastoral farming** common.

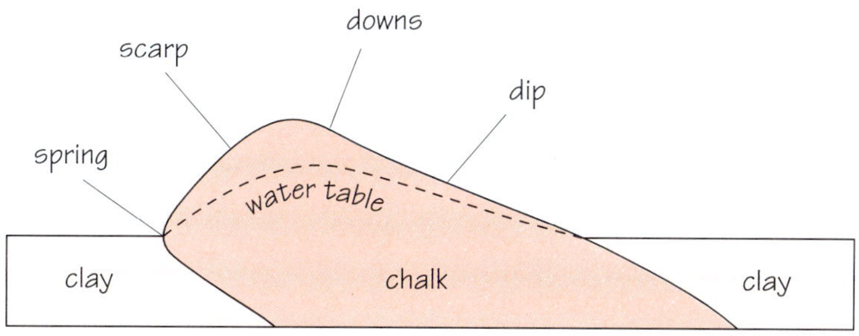

Carboniferous limestone

Carboniferous limestone – a very hard **sedimentary** rock, forming mountainous areas with steep slopes and exposed rock – called **karst** scenery – a result of limestone's **structure** and **mineral content**.

Important process.

- **Structure** – **bedding planes** and **joints**, therefore **pervious** → surface drainage rare.
- **Calcium carbonate** in limestone dissolved by rainwater seeping underground → enlarges joints and bedding planes → caves are formed.
- **Calcium carbonate** is redeposited in caves to form **stalactites** (down) and **stalagmites** (up) and **pillars** (joined).
- **Limestone pavements** formed by surface weathering along joints – forms **grikes**, and blocks, **clints**.
- **Swallow holes** form where rivers disappear underground.
- **Shake holes** form when a cave collapses.
- **Land use** includes sheep farming (thin infertile soils) and quarrying.
- **Tourism** is important dramatic scenery – popular with walkers, climbers and cavers.

Limestone scenery takes thousands of years to develop.

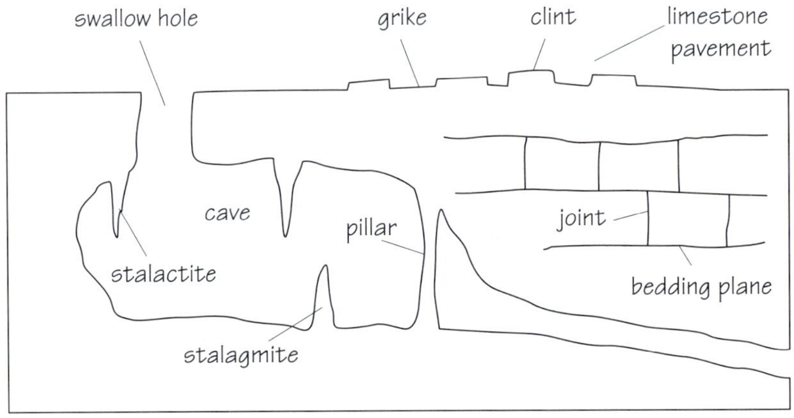

Rocks as resources

Rocks – a vital resource – many of the things we take for granted come from rocks or their minerals.

- **Granite** – weathered rock produces **kaolin** – used to make china clay, pottery and paper.
- **Limestone** – used for building stone, fertiliser, cement, and in steel making.
- **Clay** – baked to make bricks and pottery – soil for farming.
- **Chalk** – stores water underground – extracted for homes and industry.

Resource depletion

World population growth is increasing the demand for resources.

Rocks are a **non-renewable resource** – once they have been used up they cannot be replaced.
- to develop economically countries require resources – as countries become richer the speed at which resources are used up will increase
- current estimates show that silver reserves will last 20 years, gold 30 years, tin 40 years and copper 50 years – however mining companies are constantly looking for new reserves

Rock and mineral reserves may be found in **environmentally sensitive** areas – a decision has to be taken about whether to exploit the resource or to conserve it
- different groups will have different points of view – the people who live locally may object – environmental groups may be concerned about plants and animals – the mining company will stress the benefits, and want to make a profit
- LEDCs are more likely to suffer environmentally from resource exploitation – the governments need money to invest in development projects and to pay back debts to richer countries → a vulnerable position.

Rocks, resources and landscapes

Questions

1 What group of rocks is formed from magma?

2 How is metamorphic rock formed?

3 What group of rock is marble?

4 What is chalk made from?

5 What is the name for a horizontal layer in a rock?

6 What word describes a rock which allows water to pass through its joints?

7 What is 'exfoliation'?

8 What is the name of the loose material at the foot of a cliff?

9 What does 'relief' mean?

10 How did joints form in igneous rocks?

11 What features formed by weathering and erosion are found in granite areas?

12 What is a scarp slope?

13 Why are there few settlements in chalk areas?

14 How is a limestone pavement formed?

15 Why are LEDCs more likely to suffer environmentally from resource exploitation?

Rivers and water management

Rivers erode, transport and deposit material to produce distinctive landforms. Rivers provide many benefits to people but may also cause destruction.

Hydrological cycle

Hydrological (water) cycle – the continuous circling of water between the sea, atmosphere and land.

- **Evaporation** – water is heated by the sun – becomes vapour and rises.
- **Transpiration** – water vapour is released by trees and plants through **photosynthesis**.
- **Condensation** – water vapour cools as it rises and forms clouds.
- **Precipitation** – clouds release water as rain, hail and snow.
- Rivers collect and transport much of the water back to the sea.
- A **closed system** – no water is gained or lost.

Water may be stored in the system for long periods of time e.g. in a glacier, lake or sea.

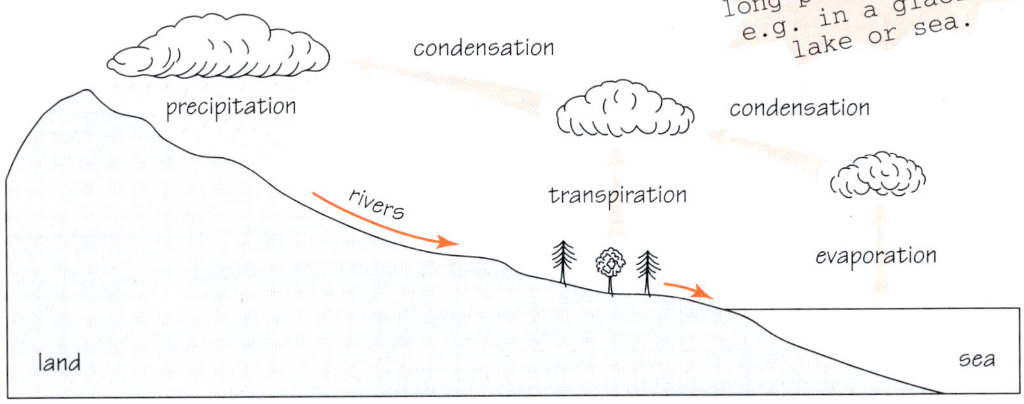

Drainage basin system

A **drainage basin** system – the 'land' part of the hydrological cycle. Precipitation follows a number of different routes to reach a river; this can be shown clearly using a **systems diagram**.

A systems diagram is a way of simplifying reality; it is divided into inputs, flows, stores and outputs.

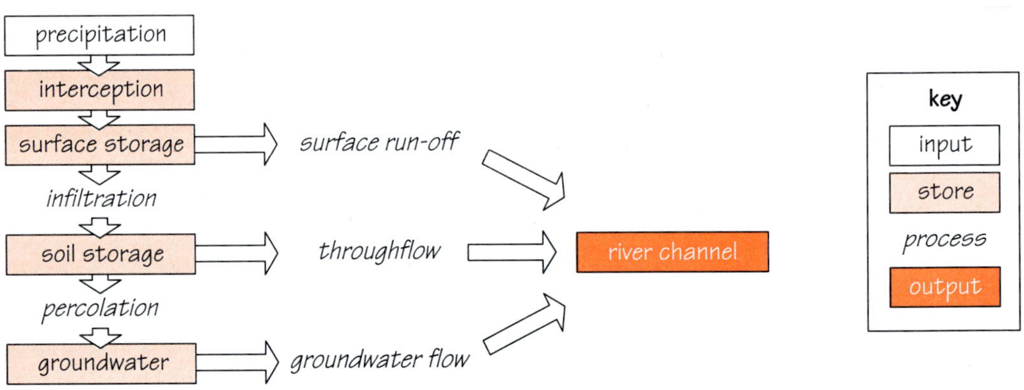

The correct terminology is worth marks for spelling, punctuation and grammar.

- **Interception** – precipitation lands on plants, trees or buildings – either runs or drips off, or evaporates.
- **Surface storage** – water lies on uneven ground – as puddles or lakes.
- **Surface run-off** – water travels as overland flow towards the river – occurs when soil is **saturated** – velocity depends on slope angle and surface conditions – rapid flow (hours).
- **Infiltration** – surface water soaks into soil.
- **Soil storage** – water is held in pore spaces in the soil.
- **Throughflow** – water flows through the soil, under the influence of gravity, towards a river – slow flow (days).
- **Percolation** – water moves downwards through the soil into permeable rocks.
- **Groundwater** – water is stored in porous rocks – saturated zone is known as the **water table**.
- **Groundwater flow** – very slow flow occurs (months) – feeds rivers and springs.
- An **open system** – water is gained from precipitation and lost through the river and evapo-transpiration.

Be clear about the difference between infiltration and percolation.

Drainage basin features

Learn this definition.

A **drainage basin** – the area of land drained by a **river** and its **tributaries** – the **catchment area** or **river basin**.

- **Watershed** – the area of high land that divides two drainage basins.

Key features of drainage basins:

- **River** – a stream of water flowing in a **channel** from high to low ground.
- **Source** – the beginning of a river.
- **Tributary** – a stream or river joining the main river.
- **Confluence** – the point where two rivers, or a river and tributary join.
- **Mouth** – the end of the river – usually the sea, though possibly a lake.

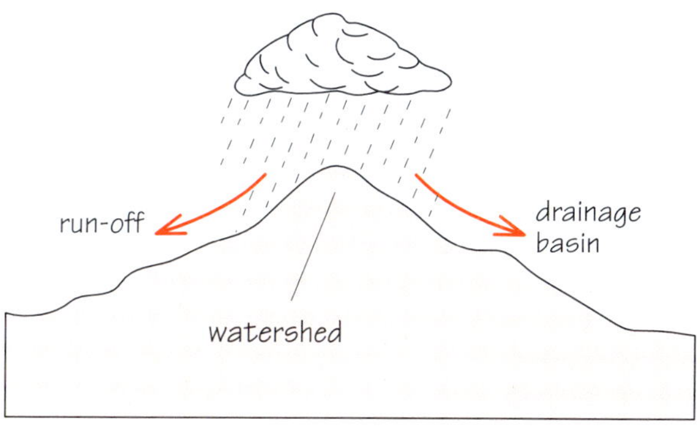

Rivers have more than one source.

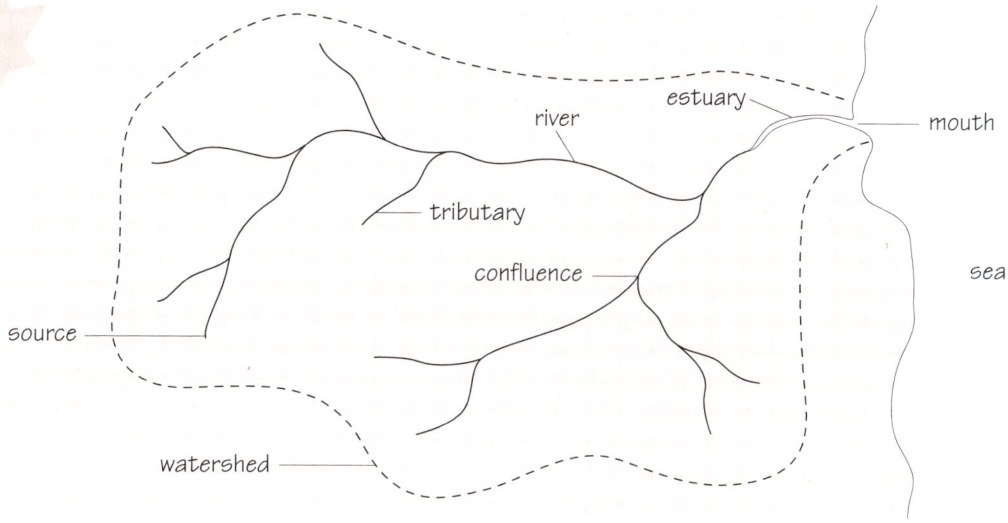

- **Long profile** of a river – a cross-section from its source to mouth – generally **concave**.
- **Gradient** decreases gradually downstream – **steep** in upper river valley, **gentle** in lower river valley.

River processes

Rivers wear away the land by **erosion** and **transport** the eroded material downstream – the eroded material (boulders, pebbles, sand and silt) are called the river's **load** – in the lower river valley the load will be **deposited**.

Processes of erosion

Don't just say 'erosion' or 'transportation', be specific about which process is happening.

Four types:

- **Hydraulic action** – force of the flowing water on the river bed and banks.
- **Corrasion / Abrasion** – material carried by the river wears away the river channel (**sandpaper effect**).
- **Attrition** – material carried by the river is broken down into smaller pieces and made rounder.
- **Corrosion** – river water is able to dissolve minerals in some rocks, e.g. limestone.

Processes of transportation

Four types:

- **Traction** – rocks and boulders rolled along river bed.
- **Saltation** – stones and pebbles bounce along river bed.
- **Suspension** – fine particles of silt 'hang' in the water – river looks murky.
- **Solution** – minerals dissolved in the river water.

Traction requires the most energy and solution the least.

Deposition

Deposition – the dropping of the river's load
– when the river slows it loses energy – it is unable to carry all the material
– the heaviest material (rocks) is deposited first and the lightest (silt) last
– the minerals in solution are not deposited but become salt in the sea.

River landforms

Created by combination of erosion, transportation and deposition – distinctive landform features are associated with different sections of the river valley.

Upper river valley

Characterised by **high land** and **steep slopes** – river flow is **turbulent** and the bedload **large** and **angular** – river erodes downwards (**vertically**) to form features such as V-shaped valleys, waterfalls and rapids.

- **V-shaped valley** – formed during periods of high flow when rivers erode vertically
  - **weathering** occurs on the valley sides → loose material is washed downstream by the river
  - **interlocking spurs** form as the river begins to **meander**.

Exam questions frequently require you to draw diagrams to explain the formation of river features.

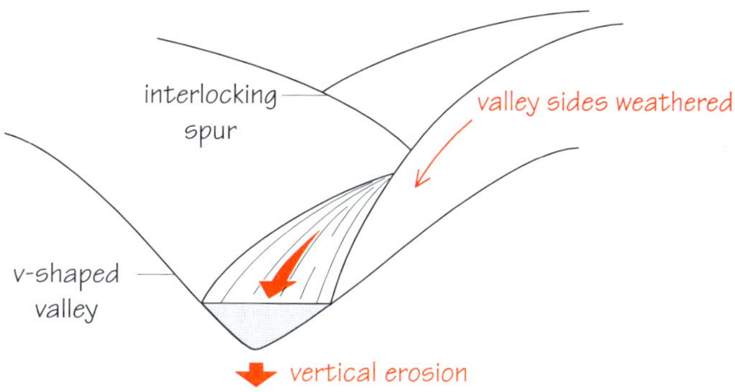

- **Waterfall** – a point along the river where water falls vertically
  - usually occur where a band of more resistant rock overlies softer rock
  - softer rock is eroded → **undercutting** the harder rock
  - **plunge pool** forms at the base
  - eventually the **overhang** of harder rock collapses
  - over a long period of time the waterfall retreats up the valley → leaving behind a steep sided **gorge**.

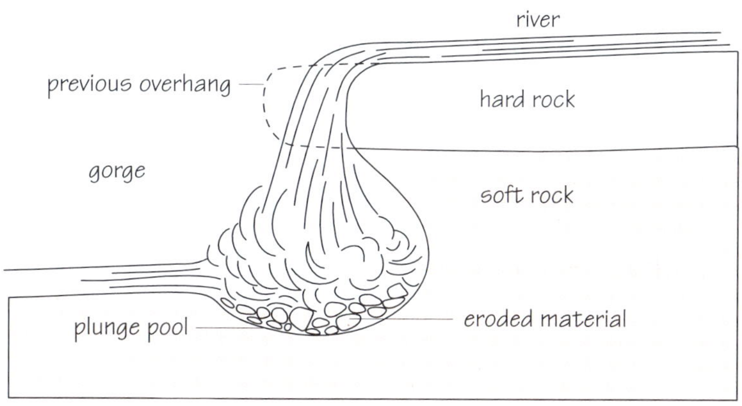

- **Rapids** – areas of turbulent water
  - caused by a sudden increase in gradient, or several bands of harder rock.
- **Potholes** – circular holes in the river bed, occuring with rapids
  - formed by pebbles eroding downwards as they are swirled around by river eddies.

Lower river valley

Characterised by **low-lying land** and a **gentle gradient** – river flow is faster and **less turbulent**, bedload is **smaller** and **rounder** – river erodes sideways (**laterally**) and deposits material to form features such as meanders, flood plains, ox-bow lakes and levées.

- **Meander** – a curve or loop in a river
  - river flows fastest on outside bend → erodes and undercuts to form **river cliff**
  - inside bend is called **slip-off slope** – slow flow causes deposition and formation of **point bar**
  - meanders move (**migrate**) downstream over hundreds of years → erosion removes interlocking spurs and carves out a flood plain.

cross-section of a meander

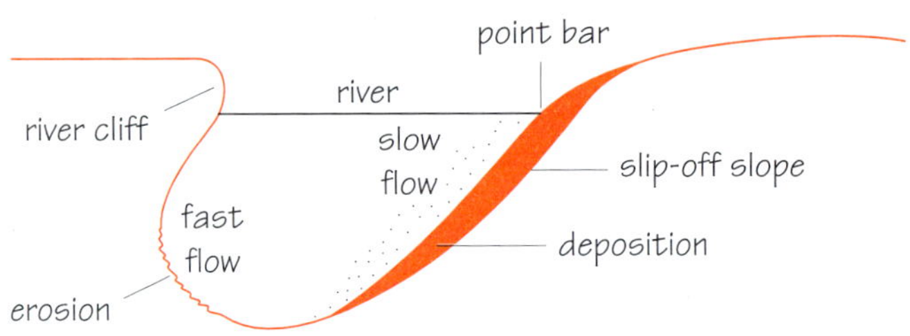

Annual flood no longer occurs where rivers are controlled by people.

- **Flood plain** – the area of flat land either side of the river channel – widened by lateral erosion and meander migration
  - annual flooding deposits layers of **alluvium** (silt) on the valley floor – as a result flood plain is gradually raised.

Ox-bow lakes gradually silt up.

- **Ox-bow lake** – a horse-shoe shaped lake lying next to a river
  - during a flood the narrow neck of land separating a looped meander is eroded
  - the river then takes the shortest route (through the new channel)
  - deposition occurs and cuts off the meander, leaving an ox-bow lake.

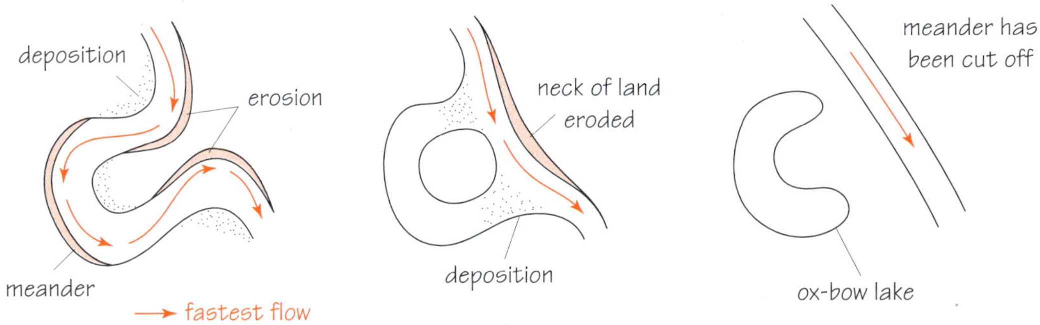

- **Levées** – raised banks of deposited material (alluvium) either side of a river
  - when a river floods, energy is quickly lost → material is deposited close to river
  - over time embankments grow in height → eventually river may flow above flood plain
  - artificial levées are built by people to control flooding.

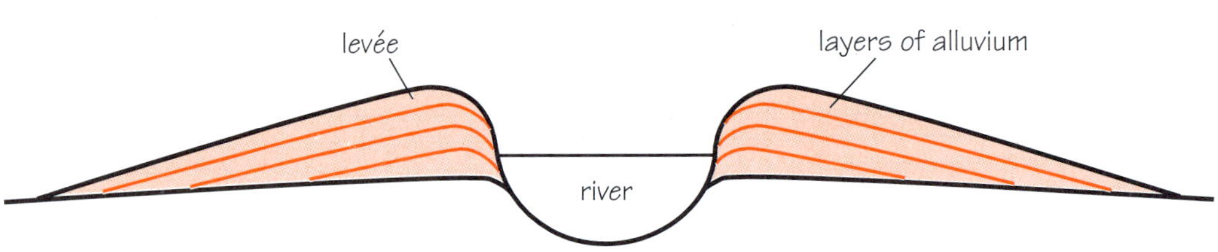

- **Braided channel** – a river which is split into a network of streams
  - occurs on rivers with an irregular flow – such as a river fed by a **glacier** or **monsoon** rains
  - during peak flow the amount of material carried by the river increases → when discharge falls rapidly the load is deposited → filling the channel with sediment.

River mouth

Tidal estuaries are shown on OS maps with a black river border.

The mouth of a river may form either an estuary or a delta.

- **Estuary** – where the river opens up into the sea
  - may be straight or funnel shaped
  - affected by the rise and fall of the tide – causes a mixture of fresh and salt water
  - deposition from the river, and sea, forms **mud flats** and **salt marshes**.

- **Delta** – a low-lying area of land which extends into the sea or lake at a river mouth
  - deposition occurs as the river loses velocity when it enters the sea or lake
  - heavy material is deposited first, and silt last → slowly a delta is built up in layers
  - **Distributaries** form as the main river channel splits into many smaller channels
  - may form different shapes – **birds foot**, **arcuate** and **cuspate**.

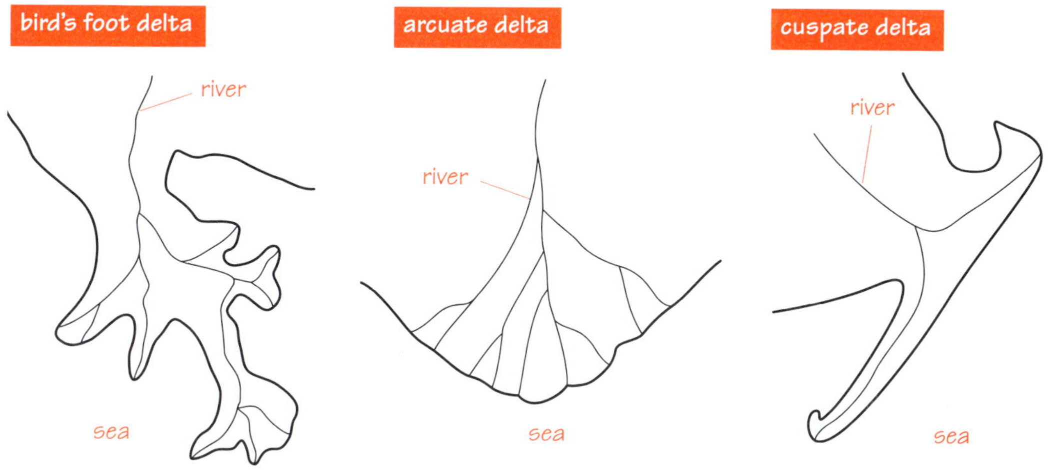

A delta will form only under certain conditions:
– the river must be transporting a large amount of sediment
– the sea must have a small tidal range and weak currents
– the sea must be shallow at the river's mouth.

How people use rivers and valleys

River valley uplands and lowlands have different land uses.

- **Settlement** occurs on floodplain – flat land.
- **Homes** and **industries** are supplied with water extracted from rivers.
- **Hydro Electric Power** (HEP) is produced by damming rivers flowing through steep valleys over impermeable rock.
- **Farming** on floodplain and deltas – fertile soil – water for **irrigation** schemes.
- **Transport** for boats and barges – movement of goods.
- **Roads** and **trains** often follow course of river in hilly areas.
- **Ports** are developed at deep river estuaries.
- **Leisure** activities such as fishing, canoeing and white water rafting.
- **Tourism** – features such as waterfalls and wildlife attract visitors.

Hydrographs

Hydrographs – show the relationship between **precipitation** and the amount of water in a river – **discharge**.

- Discharge is measured in **cumecs** (cubic metres of water per second).
- **Lag time** is the delay between maximum precipitation and peak river discharge.
- Short lag time – caused by steep slopes, impermeable rock, sparse vegetation and a small drainage basin.
- Long lag time – gentle slopes, permeable rock, dense vegetation and a large drainage basin.
- The hydrograph can be used to predict whether a river is likely to flood.

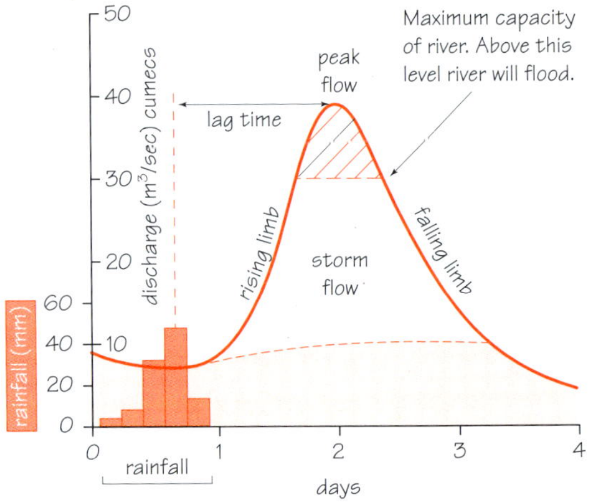

You must be able to interpret a simple hydrograph.

Flooding

Flooding – discharge too large for the channel to hold, the river 'bursts its banks'.

Causes

- **Precipitation** – heavy rainfall over a few days – saturated soil causes surface run-off.
- **Flash flood** – an intense burst of heavy rainfall in a dry area – ground is too hard for water to infiltrate → very rapid run-off.
- **Snowmelt** – as temperatures rise, snow melts → stored precipitation is released.
- **Deforestation** – reduced interception and transpiration → increases river discharge.
- **Urbanisation** – impermeable surfaces of concrete and tarmac, and drains, increase the speed and amount of surface run-off.

Impacts

- buildings and property damaged – people and animals drowned
- transport interrupted – airports closed, and road and rail networks submerged
- crops ruined – soil saturated for months afterwards
- sewage contaminates water supply – disease spreads
- economic impact on individuals, industry, government and insurance companies
- fertile silt deposited – positive impact!

The impact of flooding will be more severe in LEDCs than MEDCs.

Flood control

A number of techniques prevent, or reduce, the impact of flooding:

- **Dams** – built in the upper river valley, can control the discharge of the river.
- **Levées** – increase the height of the river banks, floodwater is contained.
- **Straightening meanders** – increases speed of river.
- **Afforestation** – increases interception and evapotranspiration, reduces run-off.
- **Spillways** – overflow channels allow river to flood low value land.
- **Early warning systems** – time to remove possessions and evacuate people.
- **Zoning** – prevent new building in areas at risk from flooding.

Flooding can be worse if a flood control technique fails.

Rivers and water management

Questions

1 What is the hydrological cycle?

2 What causes 'interception'?

3 When will surface run-off occur?

4 What is percolation?

5 What is a drainage basin?

6 What divides two drainage basins?

7 Name the four processes of erosion.

8 When does a river deposit material?

9 What processes create a flood plain?

10 What is alluvium?

11 What is a delta?

12 What does a hydrograph show?

13 What conditions will result in a short lag time?

14 How does urbanisation increase flooding?

15 How can zoning reduce the impact of flooding?

Coasts

The boundary between land and sea – **coasts** are dynamic environments which are shaped by processes of erosion, transportation and deposition. Management techniques aim to control these processes.

Coastal processes

Waves

'Swash' is a wave moving up a beach; 'backwash', a wave moving down a beach.

Waves play a very important role in shaping the coast:

- **Friction** slows down the wind as it blows over the surface of the sea → causes ripples to form.
- **Air pressure** increases as the air above travels faster and tumbles forwards → forms waves.
- **Water molecules** move in **circular** motion – not horizontally.
- **Waves break** when they reach shallow water.

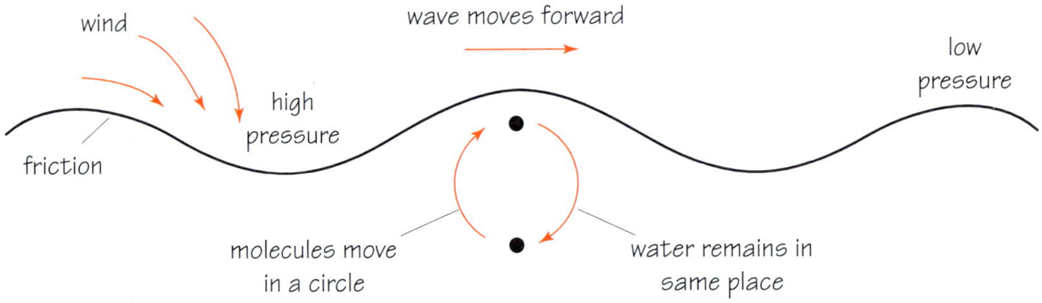

The size and energy of a wave depends on four factors:

Fetch is the most important factor.

- **Fetch** – the further a wave has travelled the larger it is.
- **Strength of wind** – the stronger the wind, the larger the wave.
- **Duration of wind** – the longer the wind blows the larger the wave.
- **Gradient of offshore sea bed** – the steeper the gradient the larger the wave.

Erosion

Four processes:

- **Hydraulic action** – the force of the waves hitting the land – compresses air trapped in cracks → increases pressure → fractures rock further.
- **Corrasion/Abrasion** – stones and pebbles in waves thrown against cliffs – sandblasting effect.
- **Attrition** – beach material is broken down into smaller pieces → becomes rounder → will eventually become sand.
- **Corrosion** – sea water slowly dissolves rocks such as limestone and chalk.

Material is transported up, down and along a beach by wave action.

Transportation

- **Swash** moves material up the beach.
- **Backwash** moves material down the beach.
- **Constructive wave** – if swash is stronger than backwash – beach material is deposited.
- **Destructive wave –** if backwash is stronger than swash – beach material is removed.
- **Longshore drift** – moves material along a beach.
  - waves approach beach at an oblique angle, break and transport material up the beach
  - backwash returns to sea at a right angle to the coast
  - material is therefore gradually transported along the beach in the direction of the dominant wind.

This is a common exam question

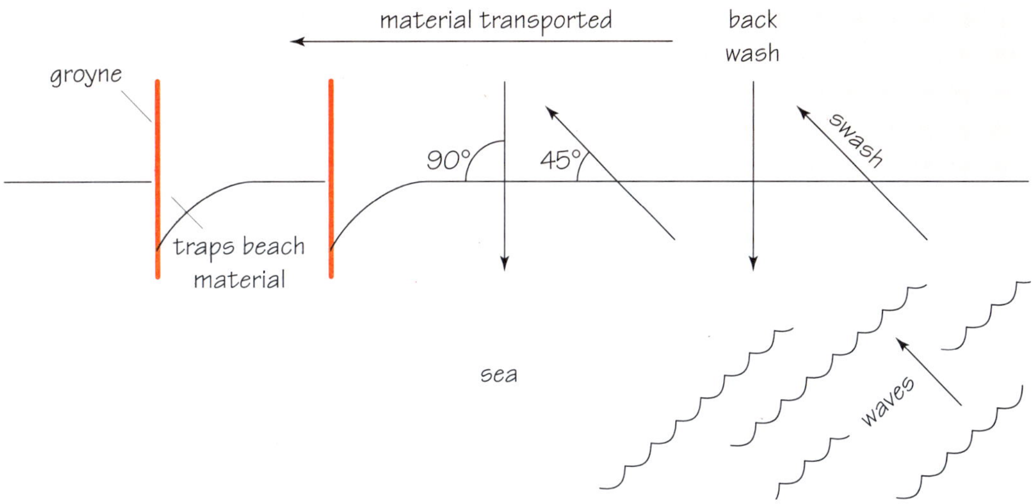

Deposition

Eroded material is **deposited** – out to sea or along the coast – to form features e.g. beaches, spits and bars.

Material transported to the sea by rivers may also be deposited on beaches.

Coastal features

Created through a combination of processes, weathering and varying geology.

Features of coastal erosion

Headlands and bays occur in areas of **Alternating bands** of hard and soft rock – typical rocks involved are chalk (harder) and clay (softer).

- **Headlands and bays**
  - **Headland** – a point of higher land protruding into the sea – formed from hard rock, resistant to erosion.
  - **Bay** – a curved break in the coastline – formed from soft rock, erodes more easily.
  - **Bayhead beaches** form when eroded material is deposited in bays.

Small bays may also form along **fault lines** in the rock – areas of weakness are eroded more quickly.

Exam questions frequently require you to draw diagrams to explain the formation of coastal features.

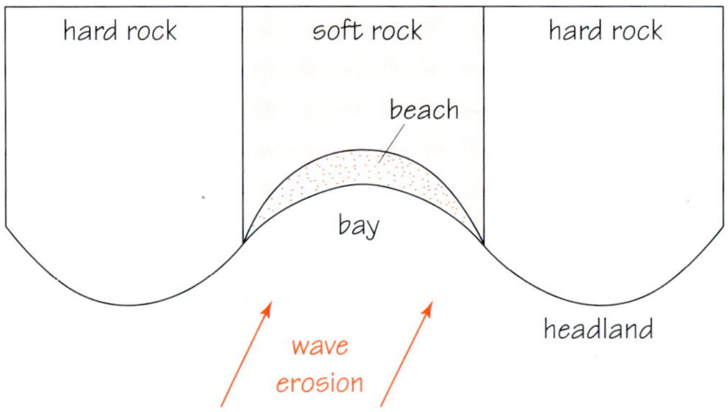

Headlands and bays.

- **Caves, arches and stacks**
  - **Fault** occuring naturally in the cliff is attacked by wave erosion.
  - **Crack** forms when a fault is widened.
  - **Cave** forms as a crack grows larger.
  - **Arch** forms as cave breaks through headland.
  - **Stack** remains as arch collapses.
  - **Stump** remains as stack is eroded and weathered.

Caves, arches, stacks and stumps are formed by long-term erosion of a narrow headland.

A **sea cave** may be connected to the cliff top by a vertical shaft called a **blowhole**.

Case Study: Swanage coast, Dorset

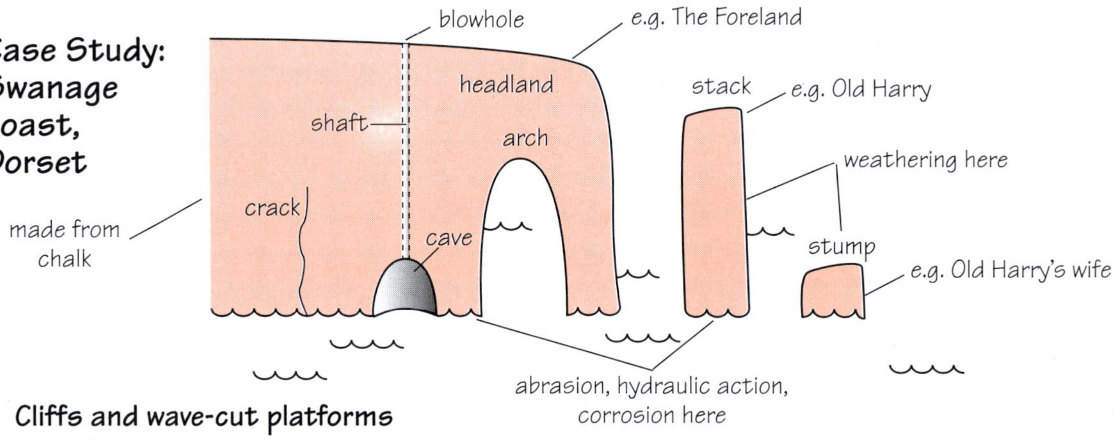

- **Cliffs and wave-cut platforms**
  - **Cliff** – wall of rock facing the sea.
  - **Wave-cut platform** – gently sloping area of rock at the foot of a cliff
    - waves erode the foot of the cliff
    - a **wave-cut notch** is formed and enlarged → cliff becomes **undercut**
    - weight of cliff above is unsupported → collapses → material removed by sea
    - cliff line retreats inland → a wave-cut platform develops at foot of cliff.

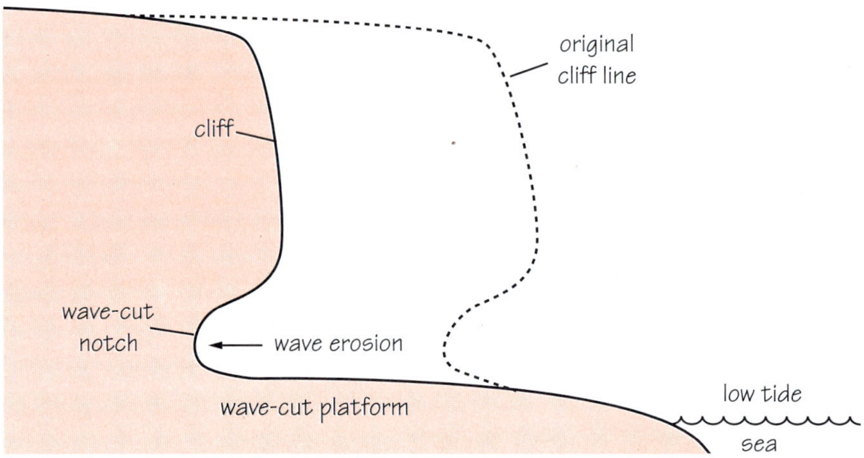

Rate of retreat and **angle** of cliff will depend on the **geology**, e.g. granite has a slow rate of retreat and a steep angle; clay retreats quickly and has gentle slopes.

Features of coastal deposition

- **Beach** – A build up of sand, pebbles and stones on a wave-cut platform
  - formed from material deposited by waves and longshore drift
  - the angle of the beach depends on the size of the beach material – a shingle beach has a steeper gradient than a sand beach.

Spits are relatively unstable and change position over long periods of time.

- **Spit** – A curved beach which extends into the sea
  - formed at a river mouth, or when the coast changes direction
  - material is transported and deposited by longshore drift
  - over many years the spit grows longer, following the direction of the **prevailing wind**.
  - **hooked end** will develop if there is an occasional **dominant wind** from another direction
  - eventually a **salt marsh** will develop in the sheltered area behind the spit.

Salt marshes are important habitats for plants and wildlife.

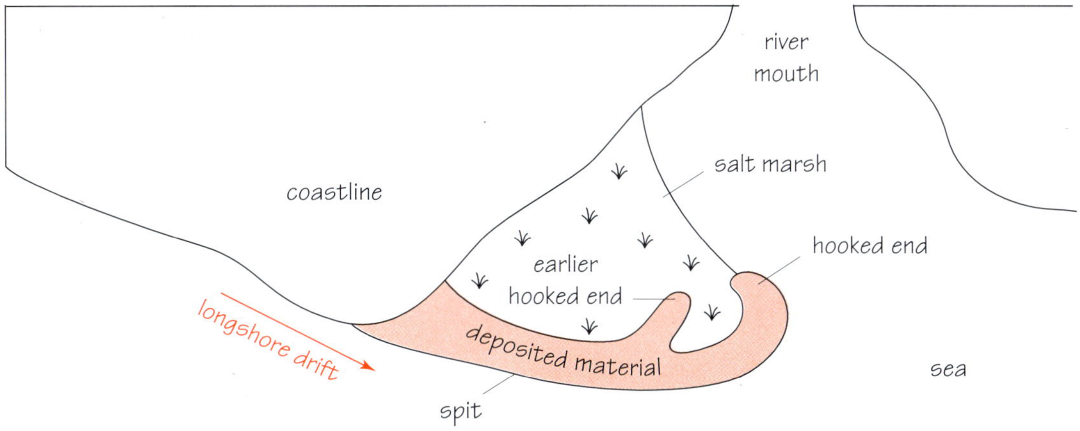

- **Tombolo** – an island joined to the land by a spit.
- **Bar** – material deposited parallel to the coast – but not touching.

Sea level changes

Over long periods of time the sea and land may rise or fall.

- In an **ice age**, when water is stored in **glaciers** and **ice sheets**, the sea falls.
- In an **interglacial period**, when glaciers melt and ice sheets retreat the sea rises.
- **Isostatic adjustment** – after an ice age, land rises as the weight of ice is removed e.g. Scotland.
- **Tectonic movements** of the Earth's crust pushes land up.

We are currently in an interglacial period.

Global warming may be causing the polar ice caps to melt – this will raise sea levels.

Features formed by sea level changes

- **Fjord** – a submerged steep sided valley which may stretch inland for many kilometres
  - formed when a **glacial trough** (valley) is flooded by an increase in sea level
  - mouth is relatively shallow as the glacier lost erosive power as it entered the sea.
- **Ria** – a submerged gentle sided valley
  - formed when a **river valley** was flooded by an increase in sea level
  - at low tide the original drainage pattern is still visible.

- **Raised beach** – an old shoreline, which is above the current sea level
  – the original cliff line and beach may be found several metres above a new cliff and wave-cut platform
  – a raised beach is formed when the land rises or sea falls.

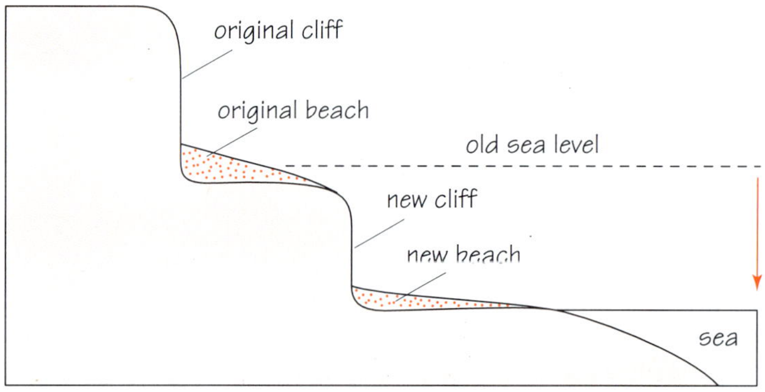

Coastal management

Many areas of coastline are at risk from erosion and flooding; if they are of high economic value several techniques may be used to manage the risk.

Management techniques

Coastal erosion is caused by a combination of **wave erosion** and **mass movement** (land slides).

- **Wide beaches** absorb wave energy – **groynes** are built on beach to trap material and build up beach – effective but deprives other areas along coast of protection.
- **Concrete sea walls** – reflect wave energy and prevent flooding – very expensive.
- **Revetments** – wooden slats allow waves through but absorb energy.
- **Gabions** – beach material wired together – unattractive – dangerous when it fails.
- **Rock armour (rip-rap)** – large boulders or concrete **tetrapods** absorb wave energy – effective but expensive and visually intrusive – especially tetrapods.
- **Beach nourishment** – beach material dredged from sea – placed on beach to replace material lost by longshore drift – may alter currents.
- **Cliff stabilisation** – improve drainage and grade cliff to a gentler slope.
- **Controlled retreat** – in areas of low economic value it is cheaper to allow erosion and compensate people for loss.

Preventing coastal erosion in one area may make it worse further down the coast.

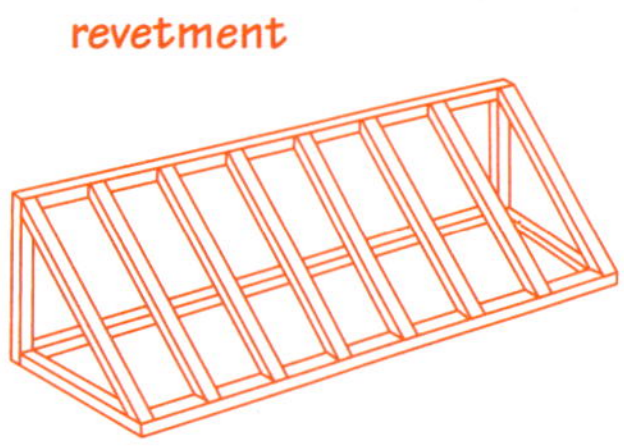

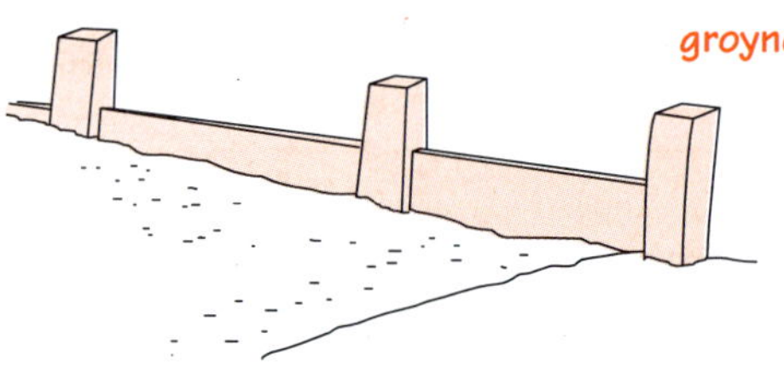

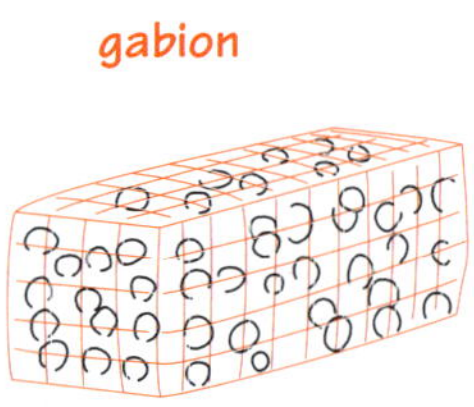

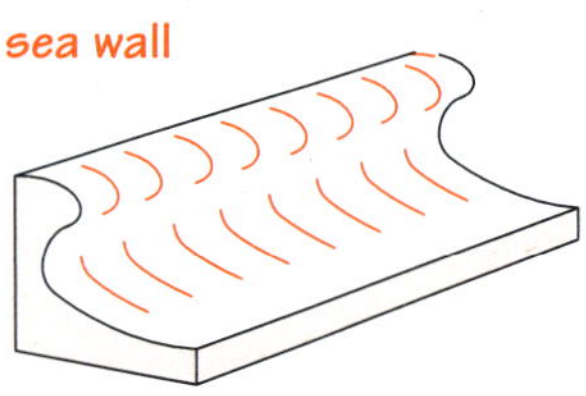

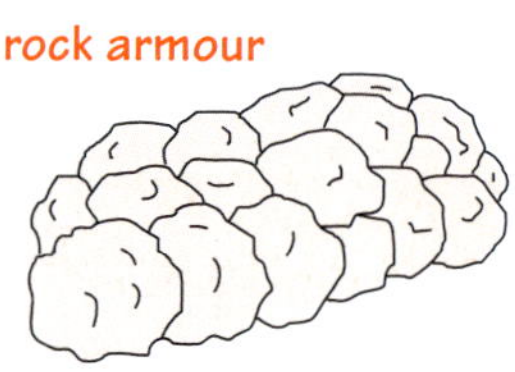

Coasts

Questions

1 What causes waves?

2 When will a wave break?

3 Which factor is the most important in controlling wave energy?

4 What types of rock are eroded by corrosion?

5 How are stones, shingle and sand moved along a beach?

6 Where do bays form?

7 What feature is formed when an arch collapses?

8 What is a wave-cut platform?

9 Which type of rock would have steeper cliffs, granite or clay?

10 Where do spits form?

11 What feature is formed in the sheltered area behind a spit?

12 Why does an ice age cause sea levels to fall?

13 What is the difference between a fjord and a ria?

14 What is a 'gabion'?

15 Why might coastal defences in one area increase erosion elsewhere?

Glaciation

Glaciation – the effects of large bodies of ice on the landscape – distinctive landforms are created by erosion and deposition – glaciated areas present opportunities and hazards for people.

The snowline is the point below which snow melts during the summer.

Accumulation is greatest in winter and **ablation** greatest in summer.

- **Glaciers** – masses of ice which form in mountain valleys
  - form when accumulation of snow is greater than rate of melting – **accumulation zone**
  - snow accumulates in upland hollows
  - compressed to form ice (**firn**)
  - eventually begins to move downhill under force of gravity
  - move an average of 2 metres per day
  - lower down the valley the glacier will begin to melt – **ablation zone**.

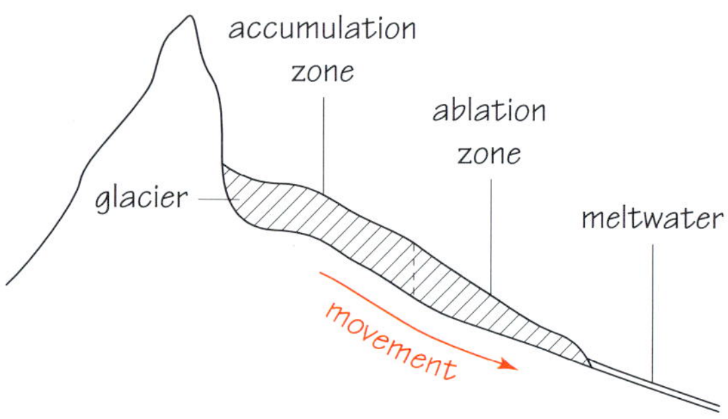

There is no land at the Arctic, only sea ice.

- **Ice sheets** – continent size masses of ice, up to 3500 metres thick
  - formation occurs at the North and South Pole – hundreds of year's snowfall
  - ice sheets move outwards from the centre in all directions.

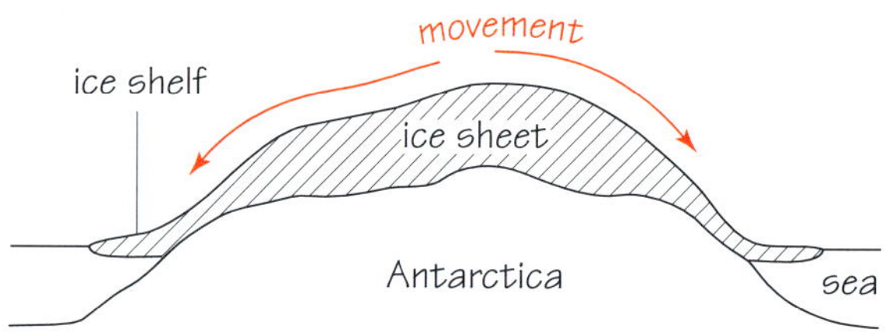

- **Time scale** – the last **glacial period** (ice age) was 30000 years ago.
  - ice sheets extended from the north and south to cover 30% of the planet
  - in the UK, glaciers grew as far south as **South Wales**, the **Midlands** and **Norfolk**.
  - 10000 years ago the ice sheets retreated – we are now in an **interglacial period**.

There are several theories but no proven explanation of why glacial periods happen.

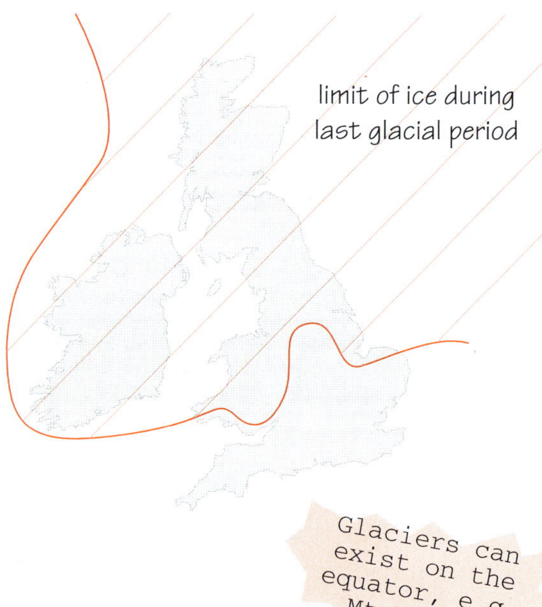

- **Location**
  - glaciers are today found in mountainous areas such as the Rockies, the Alps and Himalayas
  - ice sheets cover Antarctica and part of Greenland.

Glaciers can exist on the equator, e.g. Mt Kenya.

Glacial processes

Movement

Glaciers, although solid, are able to flow in a number of ways:
- behave as a **plastic** and bend as ice crystals slide past each other
- **melt** and **re-freeze** at the edges
- slip over water underneath the glacier – **lubrication**.

Processes of erosion

As glaciers move downhill they cause massive erosion of the land.

- **Plucking** – ice melts, then freezes around rocks and 'plucks' them away as glacier moves
- **Abrasion** – plucked rocks frozen to glacier grind away the surrounding valley – the 'sand paper' effect
- **Freeze-thaw** – above surface of glacier, water seeps into cracks in rock → freezes → expands by 9% → pressure causes rock to fracture → loose fragments fall onto glacier surface.

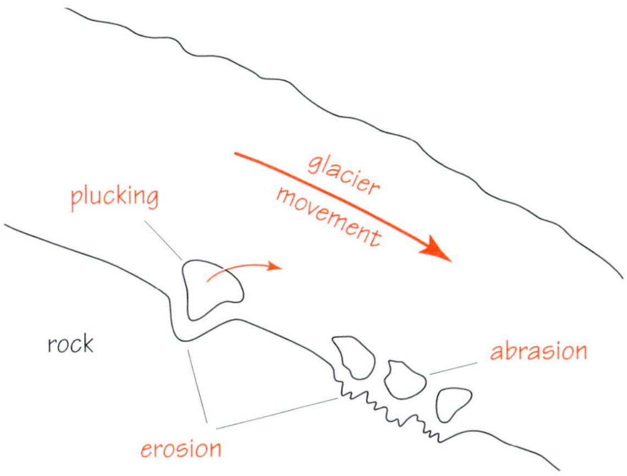

Features of glacial erosion

After glaciers have melted distinctive landforms remain.

- **Corries/cirques/cwms – deep circular hollows** near mountain tops where glaciers formed – up to 2 km across
  - steep **backwall** and sides, open front with a '**lip**'
  - formed by snow collecting in **hollows** → compacted and turned to ice → moves downhill under own weight → freeze-thaw, abrasion and plucking, steepen corrie sides and deepen floor
  - 'lip' forms at edge of corrie where there is less erosion
  - as glacier passes over lip, tension causes fractures called **crevasses**
  - today corries often contain **lakes**.

Corrie lakes may be called 'tarns'.

- **Arêtes** – **steep sided narrow ridge** between two corries in a mountain area
  - formed as the backwalls and sides of corries are weathered and eroded – distance between corries is narrowed until a 'knife edge ridge' is formed.

- **Pyramidal peaks – sharp, pointed mountain summit**
  - formed when three or more corries are weathered and eroded backwards into a mountain top, until a sharp peak is created.

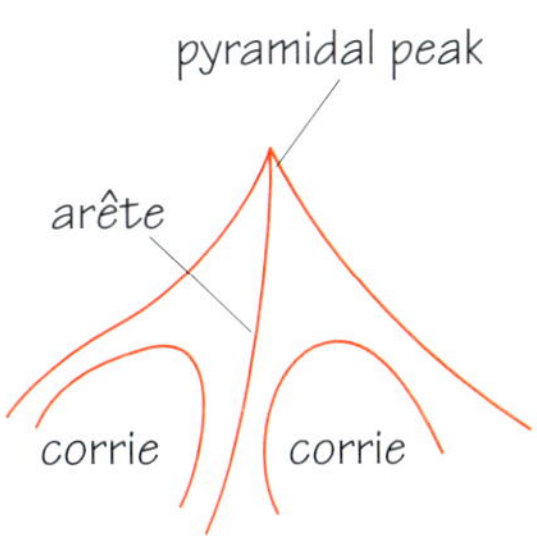

- **Glacial troughs** – **flat floored, steep sided, U-shaped valley** – also called '**U-shaped trough**'
  - formed as glaciers follow pre-glacial river valleys downhill
  - the valley is straightened and the sides and floor greatly eroded
  - tributary glaciers join main glacier – causes increase in size and erosive power.

Glaciated areas are characterised by closely grouped contour lines on OS maps.

- **Hanging valleys – a valley joining the glacial trough**, high above the floor of the main valley
  - formed when tributary glacier joined main glacier – erosive power not so great – therefore when glacier melted a sharp drop remained
  - today a river may descend as a **waterfall** from a hanging valley.

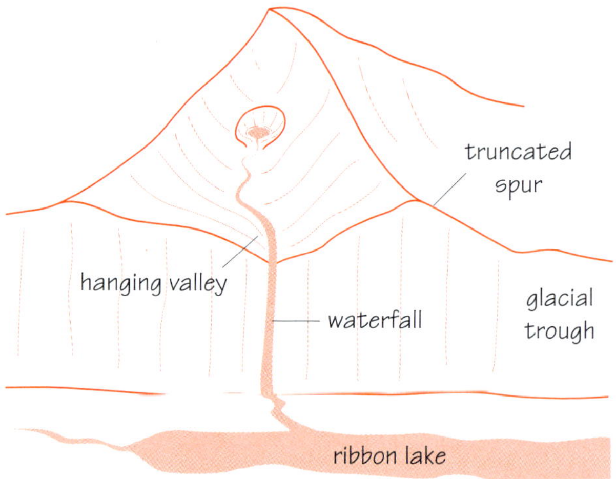

You may be asked to identify glacial features on an oblique aerial photograph.

- **Ribbon lakes – long narrow lakes** on valley floor of glacial trough
  - formed by '**over-deepening**' of valley by glacier in places (increase in power where two glaciers merged or area of softer rock)
  - after melting glacial deposits may dam the valley allowing lakes to form.
- **Truncated spurs – interlocking river spurs** which have had ends eroded to form steep cliffs
  - formed as glacier widened and deepened the original river valley.

Features of glacial deposition

'Glacial till' is more accurate term as deposits may contain no boulders and no clay!

Temperature increase will cause glaciers to melt and deposit eroded material
- deposited material is called '**glacial till**' or '**boulder clay**'
- glacial till is made up of sediment as small as fine clay and as large as huge boulders
- material deposited by the glacier remains **unsorted**
- material deposited by meltwater from the glacier will be **sorted**, clay being carried the furthest
- till forms a number of landforms.

- **Moraines** – the term given to material transported and deposited by a glacier.

Lateral moraine is deposited at the sides of the valley.
Medial moraine is deposited in the centre of the valley – formed when two glaciers converge.
Terminal moraine is deposited at the end of the glacier – the furthest point reached.
Recessional moraine forms a line of till across the valley – formed as the glacier retreated, melting stopped for a period and further deposition occurred.

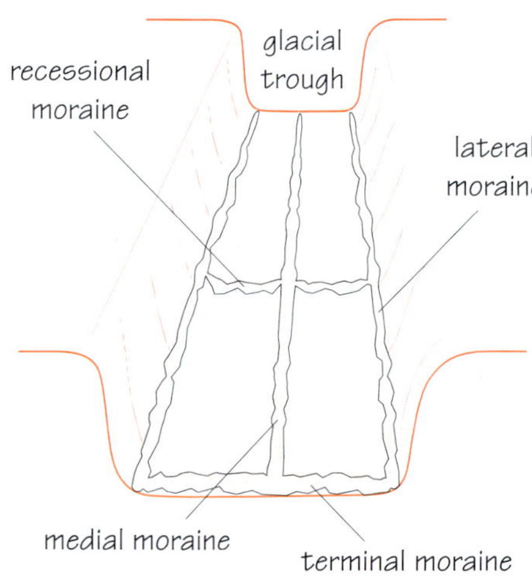

- **Drumlins – long narrow egg-shaped hills** formed from glacial till
  - occur in large numbers – **swarms** – look like a 'basket of eggs'
  - formation of drumlins is not fully understood
  - deposited by glacier but then shaped while it continued moving
  - blunt end of drumlin faces the direction of ice movement.

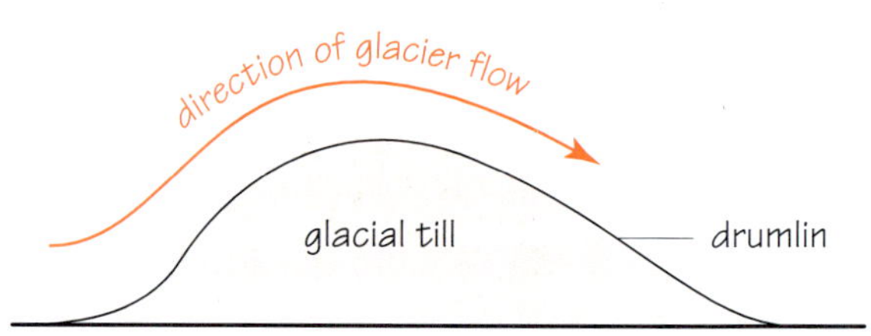

Erratics found in East Anglia came from Norway.

- **Erratics – large rocks and boulders** of a different rock type to the area in which they are found
  – have been picked up and transported to new location by glaciers and ice sheets.

Eskers, kames and outwash plains are all features of glacial meltwater.

- **Eskers – long, winding ridges of sand and gravel** between 3 to 30 metres high on valley floor
  – may be between 10 metres and 30 kilometres long.
  – formed by the deposition of material in river tunnels underneath the glacier.
- **Kames – hill or mound of sand or gravel**
  – formed when a **crevasse**, or ice cave, filled with sediment collapsed as the glacier melted.
- **Outwash plain – large area of flat land formed from glacial deposits** 'washed-out' and carried some distance by **glacial meltwater**
  – sorting of sand, gravel and clay into layers occurs.

Outwash plains may extend for hundreds of kilometres.

Human activity in glaciated areas

Glaciated regions, during interglacial periods, provide opportunities for people.

Recreation and tourism may have a negative impact on glaciated environments.

- **Recreation and tourism**
  – dramatic glaciated scenery attracts sightseers and holiday makers
  – mountains and valleys are popular with hill walkers
  – steep valley-sides attract climbers throughout the year
  – steep slopes are suitable for skiing during the winter
  – glaciated areas are often designated as **National Parks**.

Glaciated uplands and lowlands have different land uses.

- **Reservoir construction**
  – glaciated valleys often provide ideal areas to create reservoirs
  – steep valley-sides, relief rainfall and low population densities are advantages
  – reservoirs provide a water supply and reduce the risk of flooding
  – recreation opportunities such as water sports and fishing are also provided.
- **Energy supply** – glacial valleys, flooded to form reservoirs, may be used to provide **Hydro-Electric Power**
  – **waterfalls** in hanging valleys may also be harnessed as a source of energy.

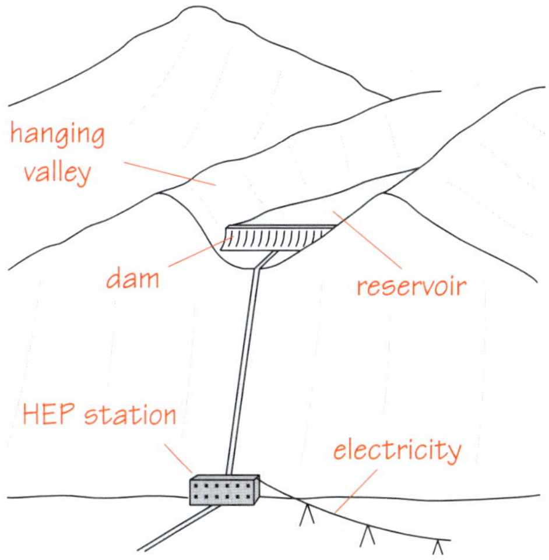

- **Farming – upland areas** are exposed to the weather and steep valley sides result in thin soils – good for pastoral farming of sheep and goats
  – **lowland areas, and outwash plains** – have large deposits of fertile till – good for arable and dairy farming, e.g. East Anglia.
- **Communications** – deep, straight valleys provide natural routeways through mountainous areas – roads and railways will be constructed on valley floor
  – fiords, flooded glacial valleys, provide natural sheltered harbours.

Glaciation

Questions

1 What is a 'glacier'?

2 What is 'firn'?

3 When did the last glacial period end?

4 Why may glaciers be described as 'plastic'?

5 What is 'plucking'?

6 Why does a 'lip' form at the edge of a corrie?

7 What landform results when two corries meet?

8 What shape is a 'glacial trough'?

9 Why are waterfalls common in upland glaciated areas?

10 What is a 'truncated spur'?

11 What causes a glacier to deposit eroded material?

12 What is a 'drumlin'?

13 Why do 'outwash plains' consist of till which has been sorted?

14 Why are glacial troughs ideal for reservoirs?

15 How have hanging valleys provided re-newable energy?

Weather and climate

Weather

All weather is powered by energy from the Sun.

Weather – the **atmospheric conditions** at a certain place and time.

The study of weather is called Meteorology.

- **Temperature** – how hot or cold the air is
  - source of heat is **solar radiation (insolation)** from Sun
  - recorded using a maximum and minimum **thermometer**
  - measured in degrees **Centigrade** (**Celsius**) or **Fahrenheit**.

Sinking air increases weight of atmosphere, therefore high pressure.

- **Air Pressure** – the weight of the atmosphere; this varies with temperature and height
  - **warm air rises** – rising air causes **low pressure**
  - **cool air sinks** – sinking air causes **high pressure**
  - decreases with height as the atmosphere becomes thinner – therefore lower at top of mountain
  - recorded using an **aneroid barometer**
  - measured in **millibars (mb)** – average pressure at sea level is 1013 mb.

Wind direction is described using the direction it has come from – if it is heading towards the north-east, it is a south-west wind.

- **Wind** – a horizontal movement of air
  - caused by differences in air pressure
  - air moves from area of high pressure (sinking) – to area of low pressure (rising)
  - the greater the difference in pressure the faster the wind
  - direction is recorded using a **wind vane**
  - speed is recorded using an **anemometer** – measured in **knots**, **kilometres** per hour or the **Beaufort Scale**.

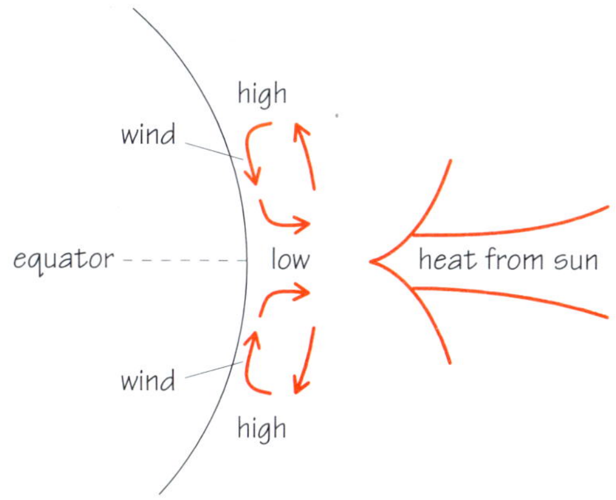

Precipitation only occurs when air rises.

- **Precipitation** – the deposition of water from the atmosphere, in any form – rain, snow, hail, sleet, frost, fog and dew
  - the atmosphere contains **water vapour** – rising vapour will cool and condense to liquid → water droplets form and grow (once over 0.5 mm diameter may fall as rain)
  - recorded using a **rain gauge** – measured in **millimetres**.

There are three types of rainfall:

Frontal rainfall occurs in **depressions**.

- **Relief rainfall** – (**orographic**) – caused by hills and mountains.
- **Convectional rainfall** – caused by warm air rising.
- **Frontal rainfall** – caused by a warm air mass and cold air mass meeting.

A **rain shadow** is the area on the lee side of a hill or mountain which receives little rain.

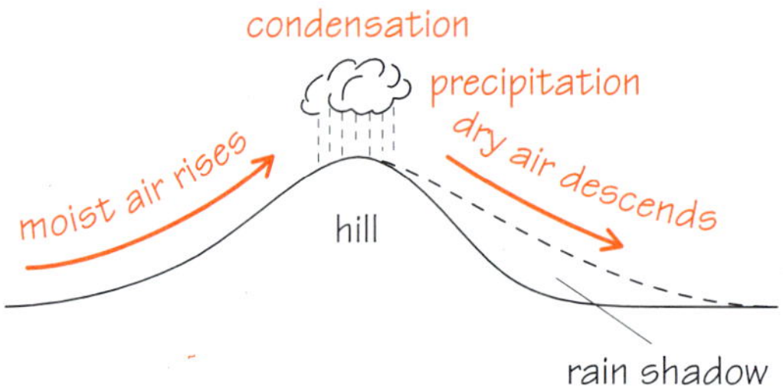

Relief

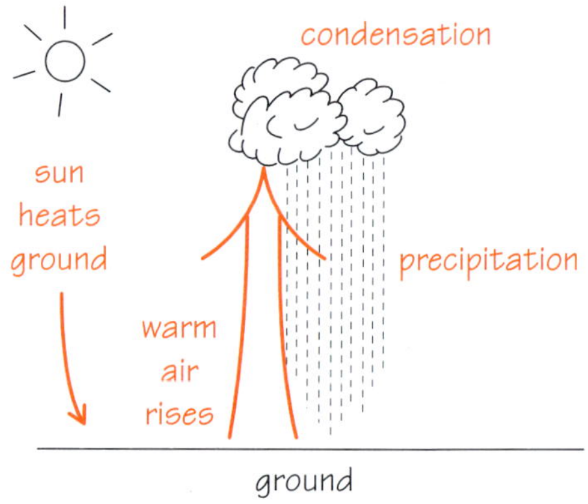

Convectional

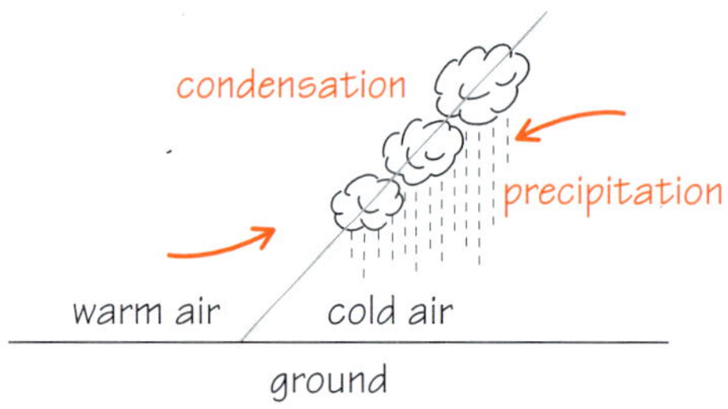

Frontal

- **Clouds** – visible masses of water droplets or ice crystals in the sky
  - as air rises it cools → water vapour condenses → clouds of droplets or ice crystals form → held in atmosphere by circulation of air.

Clouds are named by height and shape – examples in order of height include

Cirrus – wispy
Cumulonimbus – large storm clouds
Cumulus – fluffy
Stratus – flat grey
Cloud cover is measured by observation – recorded in **oktas** (eighths of sky)
Sunshine – recorded as hours per day using a sunshine recorder.

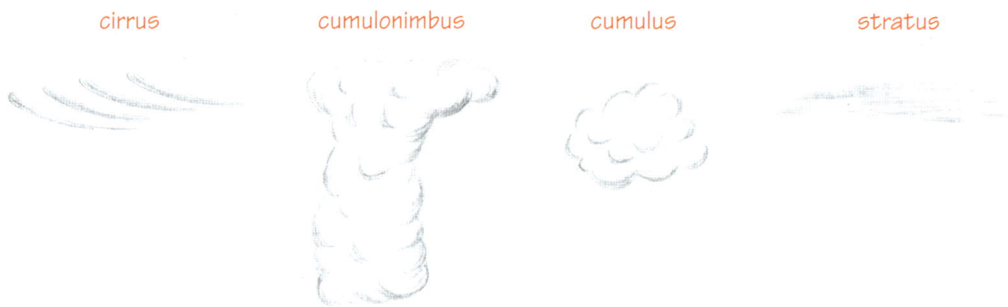

- **Relative humidity** – the actual amount of water vapour in the air, expressed as a percentage of the maximum water vapour which could be held in the air
  - the warmer the air – the more water vapour it can hold – therefore if air cools – relative humidity will increase
  - **dew point** is the temperature at which air becomes saturated and condensation begins
  - recorded with a **hygrometer**, or **wet and dry bulb thermometer**
  - measured as a **percentage**.

Weather systems

Weather factors interact to produce **weather systems** called anticyclones and depressions.

Anticyclones and depressions are common exam topics.

- **Anticyclones** – air masses of high pressure
  - air sinks → as it sinks it warms → warm air can hold more water vapour → therefore clouds unlikely to form
  - in summer anticyclones cause light winds, sunshine and high temperatures
  - in winter lack of clouds allows heat to escape at night → causes frost and cold sunny weather, sometimes causes fog
  - winds blow clockwise in the Northern Hemisphere (and anticlockwise in Southern) due to rotation of the Earth.

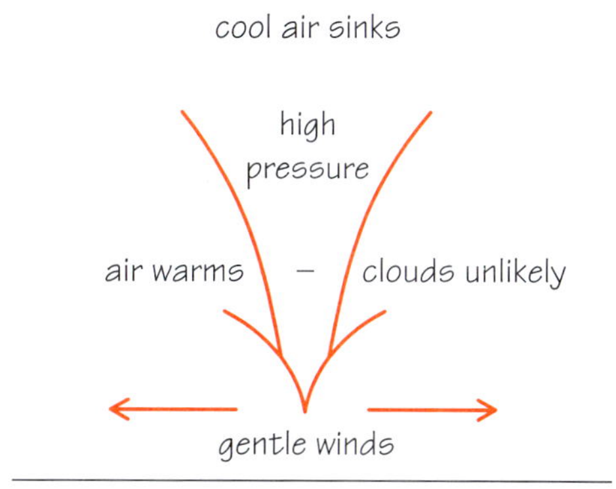

An **occluded front** is formed when warm air is completely undercut by cold air.

- **Depressions** – air masses of low pressure
  - form when a warm air mass meets a cold air mass
  - warm air mass rises over cold air mass to form a **warm front**
  - cold air undercuts warm air from behind to form a **cold front**
  - cold air causes vapour in warm air to condense → precipitation occurs along both fronts
  - air rises at the centre of a depression → draws in anticlockwise winds (in Northern Hemisphere) – the lower the pressure → the faster the winds.

Precipitation along the cold front is more intense because it is steeper.

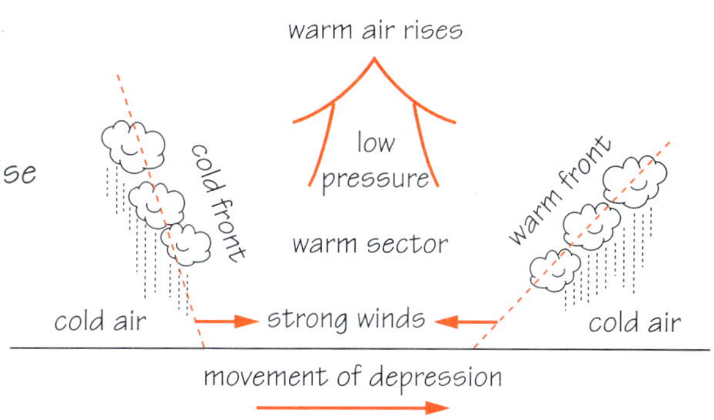

Recording techniques

Learn the synoptic chart symbols for different fronts.

- **Synoptic charts** – maps which summarise weather data for a particular time
  - data for precipitation, temperature, cloud cover, wind speed, wind direction, fronts and air pressure is represented as symbols
  - **Isobars** are lines drawn between places of equal air pressure – the closer together they are → the faster the winds.

anticyclone **depression**

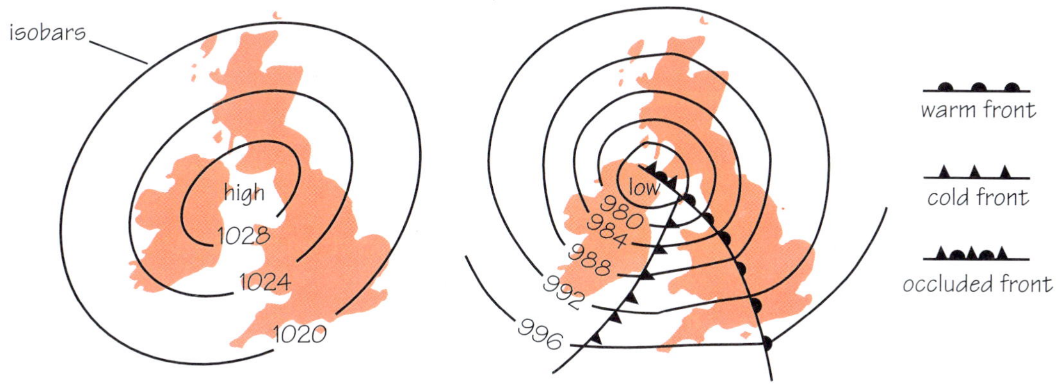

Satellite images and synoptic charts play a vital role in forecasting weather and managing weather hazards such as hurricanes and droughts.

Climate

Be clear about the difference between weather and climate.

Climate – the average weather of a place over many years; several key factors influence the climate of an area.

Factors influencing climate

Dust in the Earth's atmosphere reflects solar energy.

- **Latitude** describes how far north or south a place is from the **equator** – a major influence on climate
  - at the equator, solar energy (**insolation**) is concentrated → causes higher temperatures
  - moving north or south from the equator, solar energy is spread over a wider area and has to pass through more of the earth's atmosphere → less concentrated → lower temperatures
  - temperature and day length vary throughout year due to latitude and the tilt of the earth as it rotates around the sun (every 365¼ days) – the hemisphere which is tilted towards the sun experiences summer, while the other experiences winter.

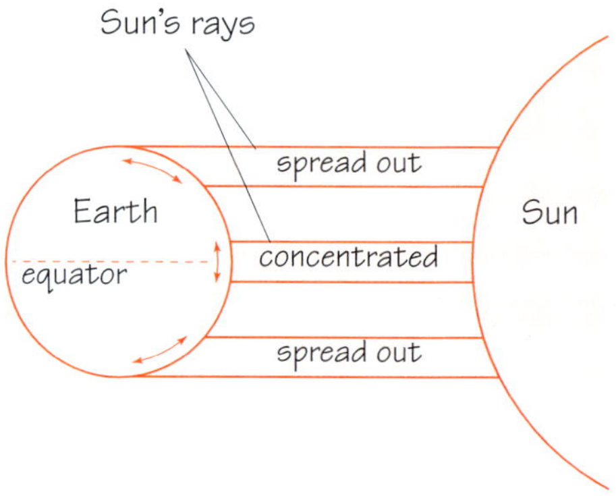

- **Altitude** – the distance from the Earth's surface – the sun's energy is **absorbed** and **radiated** as heat by the Earth's surface
  - atmospheric gases including **water vapour**, **carbon dioxide** and **methane** absorb the heat
  - the atmosphere is most dense at the Earth's surface, therefore absorbs much heat
  - as **altitude** increases, density of atmosphere decreases – therefore absorbs less heat
  - temperatures fall by 6.5 °C every 1000 metres of altitude (known as **lapse rate**).

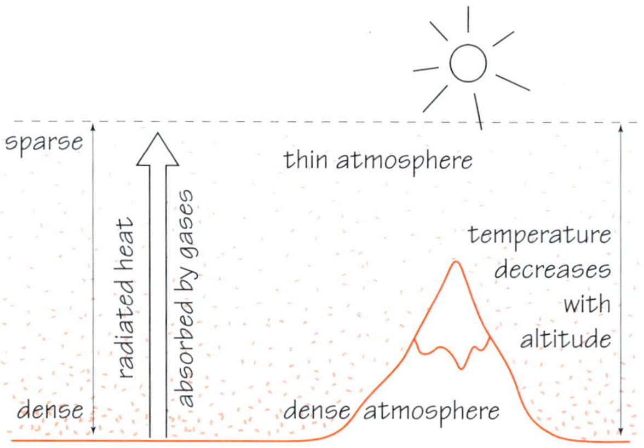

Coastal areas tend to receive more rainfall than inland areas due to evaporation from the sea.

- **Distance from sea**
  - the sea absorbs and stores heat at a greater depth than land – therefore the sea is slow to heat up and cool down, whereas the land heats up and cools down quickly.
  - in winter, coastal areas are kept warmer by the sea, but in the summer, they are kept cooler
  - a **maritime** or **oceanic climate** has a relatively small annual temperature range
  - large inland areas not influenced by the sea – **continental climates** – experience hot summers and cold winters – a large annual temperature range.

- **Prevailing wind** – the most frequent – affect temperature and precipitation
  - sea winds bring precipitation
  - land winds bring dry weather
  - polar winds bring cold weather
  - tropical winds bring warm or hot weather.

The prevailing wind for the UK is from the south-west.

- ***Ocean currents*** – movements of warm or cold water through the oceans
  - **Warm currents** moving from the tropics towards the poles warm the surrounding area, particularly in winter.
  - **Cold currents** usually have less effect, but may lower temperatures.

Climatic regions

The world may be classified into different **climatic regions** – four examples are given below.

UK climate – maritime

The **UK** is located between 50° and 60° north of the equator and has a **maritime climate**

Make sure you can explain the temperature differences between summer and winter.

- in July (summer) the average temperature in the north is 13 °C – this increases to 17 °C in the south – due to **latitude**
- in January (winter) the coldest place is the north-east, averaging 3 °C – temperatures increase towards the south-west, averaging 7 °C – caused by the warming influence of the **North Atlantic Drift** (warm ocean current from Florida) and warm south-west winds.

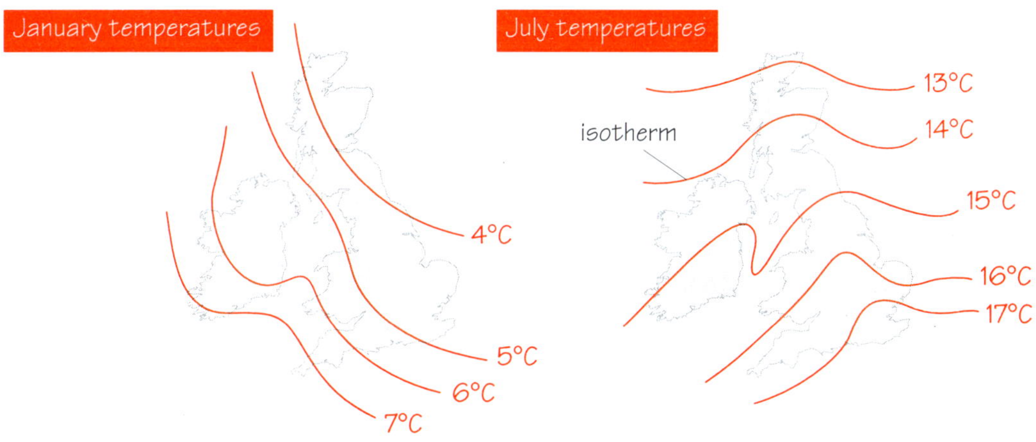

- **Tropical** and **polar** air masses meet and form depressions which approach from the west
- precipitation falls throughout the year but is distributed unevenly
- areas on the west coast receive over 2000 mm – areas on the east coast only receive up to 750 mm – prevailing winds from south-west (moist) are forced to rise by mountains on west coast – causes **relief rainfall** – areas east of mountains are in **rain shadow**.

Continental climate

These occur inland in **North America** and **Eurasia** between 35° and 60° north

- precipitation is low due to distance from sea – average 500 mm per year
- maximum precipitation occurs in summer due to convection → thunderstorms

– temperatures average 18 °C in summer and –19 °C in winter – an annual range of 37 °C → caused by continentality → land heats up and cools down quickly → no influence from sea.

Equatorial climate

Cloud cover limits temperature in equatorial regions.

There is little seasonal change in equatorial climates.

These occur mainly between 5° north and south of the equator
– precipitation is caused by **convection** – heats up during morning → rains in afternoon – average 2000 mm to 5000 mm per year
– temperatures average 26 °C all year – low latitude therefore sun overhead all year.

Desert climate

Climate graphs show precipitation as bars and temperature as a line.

Temperature range within a day is called '**diurnal range**'.

These usually occur between 10° and 30° north or south of the equator – have a hot and cool season as the position of the sun changes over the year
– defined as having less than 250 mm of precipitation per year, however some have had no rain for many years
– form in areas where air is **descending** (high pressure) and where the prevailing wind blows across land → air is dry and as it sinks it warms → therefore no clouds
– temperatures during the day may exceed 50 °C but at night drop as low as 5 °C – these extremes occur due to lack of clouds → heat is able to escape.

Weather hazards

Extreme weather conditions create **hazards** for people, e.g., gales, tropical storms, tornadoes, snow, ice storms, fog and drought; the impact will vary depending on an area's level of development.

A tropical storm has short-term and long-term impacts.

- **Tropical storms** – huge depressions which form over oceans in the tropics when sea temperature exceeds 27 °C – late summer/autumn – known as **hurricanes**, **cyclones** and **typhoons**
  – heat causes massive evaporation → vapour rises, cools, condenses → heavy rain falls → releases more heat to power storm
  – **intense low pressure** develops → 200 kph winds are drawn upwards in a spiralling motion
  – tropical storms may grow to over 500 km across and last several days, travelling slowly in a westerly direction – at centre of hurricane is calm '**eye**' of sinking air
  – intense low pressure causes sea to rise → causing **storm surge** and flooding of coastal areas
  – on reaching land a hurricane causes flooding due to heavy precipitation and destruction of buildings due to powerful winds; lives may be lost
  – a hurricane will decay when it is cut off from the sea.

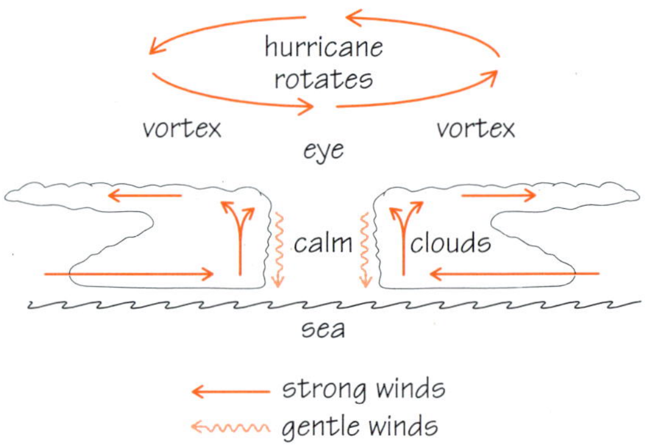

Weather and climate

Questions

1 What is the difference between weather and climate?

2 Does sinking air cause high pressure or low pressure?

3 What causes wind?

4 What causes frontal rainfall?

5 What is relative humidity?

6 What is an anticyclone?

7 Is air rising or sinking in a depression?

8 What is an occluded front?

9 How is air pressure shown on a map?

10 If it is 20 °C at sea level, what will the temperature be 4000 metres up a mountain?

11 Why is the south-west of the UK relatively warm in winter?

12 Why does the east coast of the UK not receive much rainfall?

13 Where do equatorial climates occur?

14 Why are deserts very cold at night?

15 What conditions are necessary for hurricanes to form?

Human Geography

Population and migration

Population

The number of people living in the world, or an area such as a country is its population. Some areas of the world are crowded, others have few people. Population changes such as growth, decline and migration create benefits and problems.

Population distribution

- **Population distribution** – describes how people are spread out over an area, region, country or the world.
- **Population density** – describes how crowded an area is → the number of people per km^2.

Be clear about the difference between population distribution and density.

$$\frac{\text{population}}{\text{area } (km^2)} = \text{population density}(km^2)$$

- **Densely populated** – an area is considered crowded – over 200 people per km^2.
- **Sparsely populated** – an area has few people – less than 10 people per km^2.
- **UK average population density** – 233 people per km^2 → total population 57 million – total land area 245 000 km^2.
- **World average population density** – 43 people per km^2.

Always include the units in a numerical answer.

Global population distribution

Population is distributed very unevenly across the world
- the majority live on only one third of the world's land surface
- densest areas include Western Europe, Eastern USA, India and China
- sparsest areas include Canada, North Africa, Australia and Brazil.

Population distribution is usually shown using a **shaded (choropleth) map** – this hides local variations and does not show gradual changes.

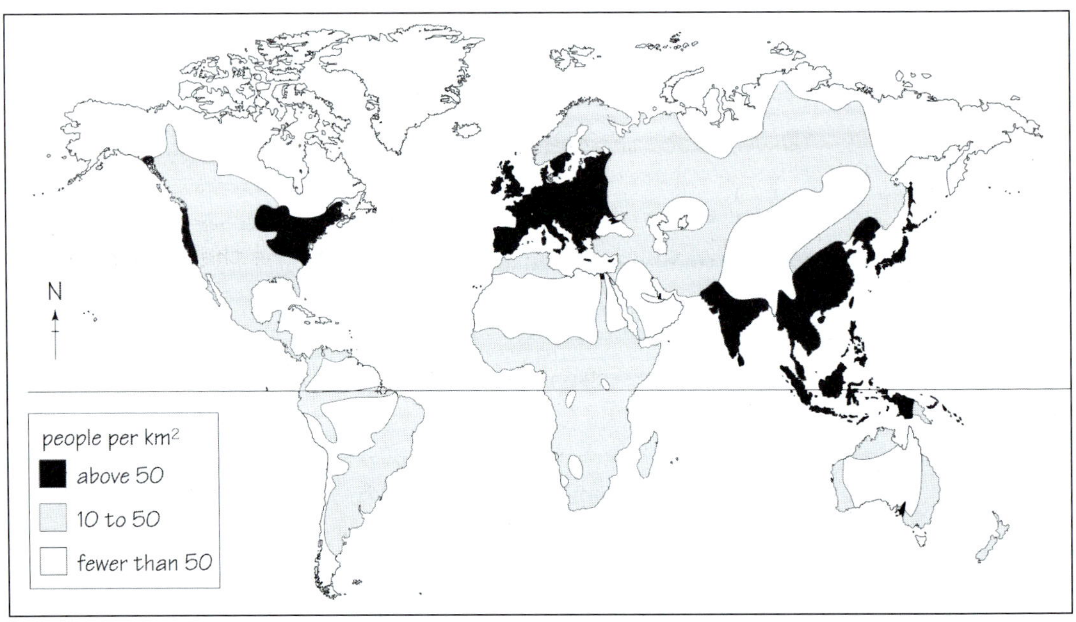

Economic, political and historical factors are important on a regional scale.

Influences on population distribution

There are several factors which together explain why the world's population is unevenly distributed.

- **Relief** – mountainous areas are too cold → farming is not possible – no roads.
- **Climate** – regular precipitation is needed to supply homes, industry and agriculture with water; low temperatures limit agriculture.
- **Vegetation** – dense forest areas limit access → low density.
- **Soils** – fertile soils produce good crops → can support high density.
- **Resources** – raw materials such as coal led to industrial development and high population densities – today less important due to imports.
- **Economic** – industry and offices attract people → cities develop.
- **Political** – government decisions such as the location of the capital city.
- **Historical** – areas settled for longest have higher population densities.

Population growth

Statistics

In 1800 the world population reached 1 billion people; today the population of the world is about 6 billion

– this figure is now growing at an **exponential rate** – it doubles every 50 years

– world population is expected to reach up to 12 billion by 2050 – after which it may stabilise

– this rapid increase in population is sometimes called the '**population explosion**'

– population growth is not equally distributed around the world – 95% of the growth is occurring in LEDCs

– some of the fastest growing areas are sub-Saharan Africa (3%), Central America (2.4%), and India (2%)

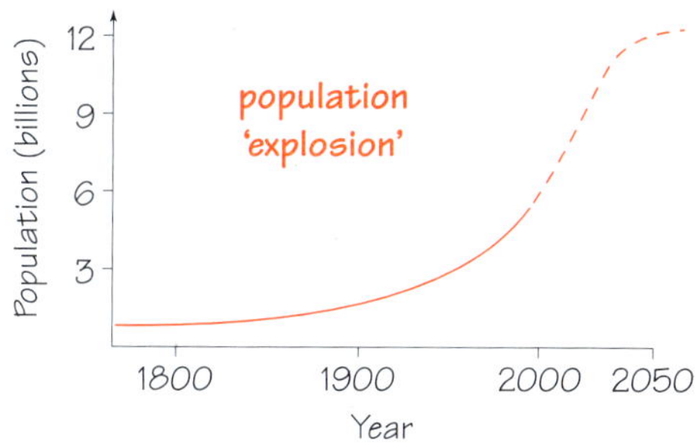

– MEDCs have reached a '**replacement level**' of population growth or are experiencing a **decrease**.

Causes of population growth

Birth and death rates are expressed as rates per 1000 to allow comparisons between countries.

World population growth has been caused by birth rates exceeding death rates.

- **Birth rate** – the number of births per thousand people in a year.
- **Death rate** – the number of deaths per thousand people in a year.
- **Natural increase** – if there are more births than deaths the population will grow – expressed as a percentage per year – world average is 1.5%.

If there are more deaths than births, the population will decrease.

$$\frac{\text{birth rate} - \text{death rate}}{10} = \text{natural increase}$$

International migration will also have an effect on the population of individual countries.

Demographic transition model

A common exam question. You must be able to explain these four stages in detail.

The **demographic transition model** represents the changes that have occurred in birth rates, death rates and population growth.

The model explains population change in four stages:

1 **High stationary** – birth rates high → no birth control, children needed for labour/death rates high – poor hygiene, disease = population grows slowly.
2 **Early expanding** – birth rates stay high/death rates fall → industrialisation begins → improved sanitation, healthcare and diet = rapid population growth.
3 **Late expanding** – birth rates fall → birth control, increased wealth, improved rights for women/death rates fall slightly = slow population growth.
4 **Low stationary** – birth rates low/death rates low = fluctuating but steady population.

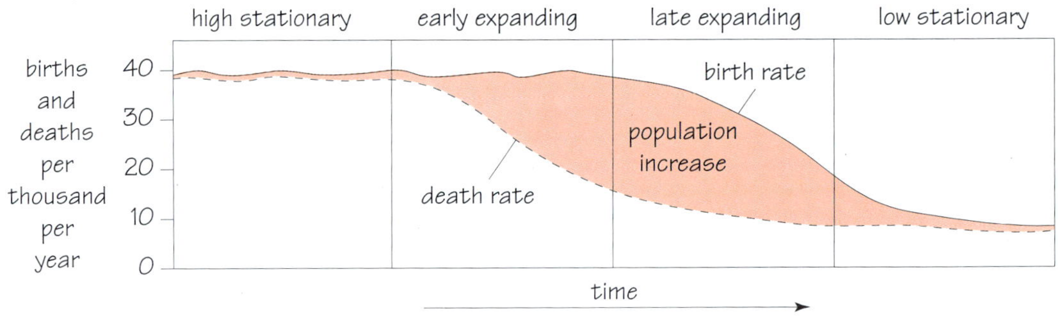

The model was designed to show how all countries change **demographically** – it is now accepted that some things were not considered.

- **LEDCs** which have not industrialised may still experience a stage 2 fall in death rates due to improved health care, sanitation and water supply.
- **MEDCs** are entering a fifth stage where death rates exceed birth rates and population is falling.

Overpopulation

What is considered a 'reasonable' standard of living will vary between cultures.

Overpopulation – a consequence of rapid population growth
– occurs when the **resources** and **infrastructure** of an area are not sufficient to provide people with a 'reasonable' standard of living
– resources and infrastructure – land, energy, food, clean water, housing, jobs, education and healthcare
– consequences in a LEDC – poverty, hunger, diseases e.g. cholera and diarrhoea, squatter settlements due to housing shortages and desertification from overgrazing
– consequences in a MEDC – traffic congestion and loss of countryside for housing developments
– MEDCs are able to support high populations at a better standard of living because they can afford to import resources from LEDCs
– global consequences – deforestation, global warming and acid deposition.

Population control

Controlling population growth – vital to ensure a sustainable future for the Earth.

Be able to explain each reason.

Understanding high birth rates

People in a large number of LEDCs have many children for several reasons:

- **Labour** – children are needed to work on the land or in factories to provide income.
- **Old age** – with no pensions, people rely on their children to support them in old age.
- **Infant mortality** – many babies die due to poor health care → need to have several to ensure some survive to adulthood.
- **Lottery factor** – the more children you have, the more chance of one becoming successful and making a lot of money.
- **Religion** – some religions, such as Catholicism, do not approve of contraception.
- **Status** – both men and women may gain status by having a lot of children.

Population control is an issue on which different groups of people have strong opinions.

Reducing birth rates

To reduce birth rates it is vital to understand the reasons above; contraception alone will not work.

- **Status** – the most successful way to reduce birth rates is to raise the status of women – in many cultures the husband decides how many children they have.
- **Education** – educating women helps to achieve this → especially learning about family planning.
- **Healthcare** – immunisation of babies reduces the infant death rate → fewer children needed.
- **Marriage** – raising the legal marriage age reduces the number of children born to a woman.
- **Advertising** – attitudes can be changed through massive advertising campaigns.
- **Financial** – offer bonuses to families who limit their number of children.
- **Force** – laws limiting the number of children, e.g. China → maximum one child per family.

Population structure

Population structure – the make up of a population in terms of **age**, **sex** and **life expectancy**; usually shown as a population, or age-sex, pyramid.

Population pyramids

Population pyramids are used to plan service provision, e.g. number of hospitals and schools needed.

Population pyramids – horizontal bar graphs with:
– the population divided into five year age groups → shown as a percentage of the total population
– males on the left – females on the right
– trends in the population structure of a country can be identified – birth rate, infant mortality rate, death rate, and life expectancy
– LEDCs and MEDCs have different shaped pyramids.

LEDC pyramid

You must be able to interpret population pyramids.

- **Wide base** = high birth rate → high percentage of children.
- **Steep sides** = high infant mortality rate and death rate.
- **Narrow peak** = short life expectancy.

LEDC pyramid

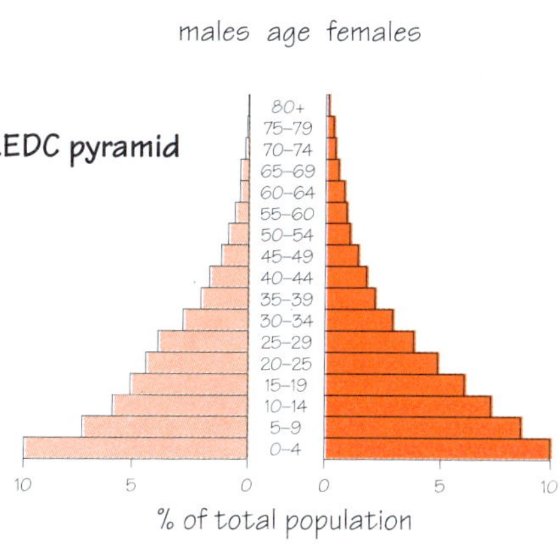

MEDC pyramid

- **Narrowing base** = low and falling birth rate → low percentage of children.
- **Vertical sides** = low infant mortality and death rate.
- **Wide peak** = long life expectancy.

MEDC pyramid

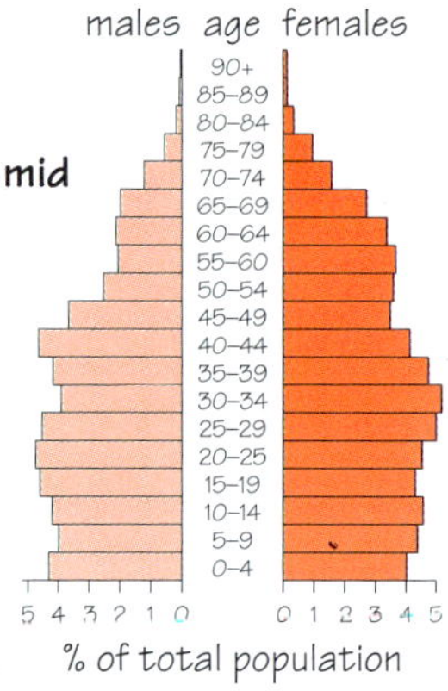

Age dependency

The young and old in a population are supported financially by the economically active
– the **economically active** (workers) are considered to be between 15 and 65 years old
– LEDCs have a high percentage of children – **young dependants**
– MEDCs have a high percentage of elderly people – **elderly dependants**
– a high number of dependants can create economic problems for a country
– the ageing population in MEDCs is being supported by a declining number of workers – has implications for pensions and services such as hospitals.

Migration

Migration is the movement of people from one area to another
– may be **permanent, seasonal** or **temporary**
– may be **internal** (within the same country) or **international** (from one country to another)
– may be **forced** or **voluntary**
– **immigration** is the movement into a country
– **emigration** is the movement out of a country
– most migrants are young adults.

International migration is subject to immigration laws – most countries discourage migrants.

Causes of migration

The causes of migration can be divided into push and pull factors.

- **Push** factors encourage or force people to leave.
- **Pull** factors attract people.

Possible **push** factors

- Crop failure
- Volcanic eruption
- Limited education
- War.

Possible **pull** factors

- Job opportunities
- Area safe from natural hazards
- Free schooling
- Better medical care.

Rural to urban migration

Rural to urban migration – the movement from the countryside to cities
– **urbanisation** is happening mainly in LEDCs
– push factors – few jobs, poor wages, poor health care and few education opportunities
– pull factors – jobs in factories, higher wages, clinics, more schools and glamour of city life.

Urbanisation is an increase in the percentage of people living in cities.

Impacts

- **City** – life for migrants in reality is hard → little paid employment, lack of services, and squatter settlement housing.
- **Countryside** – becomes depopulated → reduced food production, population structure dominated by women and elderly.

Urban to rural migration

Counter-urbanisation – the movement from cities back to the countryside – is happening mainly in MEDCs
- push factors – lack of open space, noise, air pollution, traffic congestion and fear of crime
- pull factors – attractive countryside, safer to bring up children, larger houses and improved transport makes commuting possible.

Impacts

- **Inner city** – becomes depopulated → housing empty and boarded up → services decline.
- **Countryside** – under pressure for new housing developments → possible friction between locals and newcomers.

International migration

Migrants tend to be concentrated in inner city areas where there is cheap housing.

Voluntary **international migration** is usually for economic and social reasons – people are seeking a better standard of living and/or wish to be with relatives.
- **Impacts on receiving country** – may place a strain on the infrastructure → jobs, schools, hospitals → however migrants may be skilled, or provide cheap labour and benefit the economy.
- **On migrants' home countries** – lose economically active population, leaving elderly dependants → however money sent back by migrants may help support the economy.

Refugees

There are over 17 million refugees in the world.

Refugees – migrants who have been forced to leave an area or country due to environmental or political problems, such as flooding, war or persecution
– most move to LEDCs, placing even greater strain on the infrastructure
– may be blamed for taking jobs and housing → leads to resentment and racism
– governments have a difficult job to decide if migrants are genuine refugees
– many are skilled and will benefit their new country.

Population and migration

Questions

1 What does population distribution mean?

2 Why is a choropleth map of population density inaccurate?

3 What is exponential population growth?

4 Why are birth and death rates expressed as rates per 1000?

5 Why are MEDCs described as 'entering a fifth stage'?

6 Why are MEDCs able to support higher populations?

7 How can improving the status of women reduce birth rates?

8 What is a population structure?

9 Explain the unusual shape of pyramid A.

A

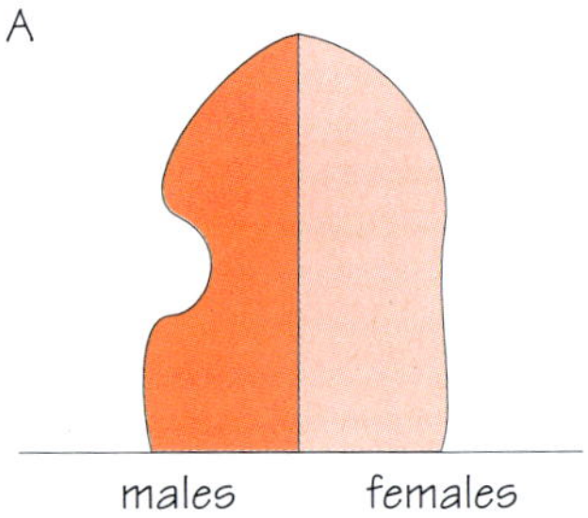

10 Who are the 'economically active' in a population?

11 What is rural-urban migration?

12 What is urbanisation?

13 What is counter-urbanisation?

14 Why do migrants sometimes experience racism?

15 What is a refugee?

Settlement and urbanisation

Settlement

Settlement began 10000 years ago when nomadic people learned to cultivate crops. A settlement is a place where people live, ranging from a single house to a city; these settlements may be classified using a number of different criteria.

Site

You may be asked to annotate a map to explain the site of a settlement.

Site – the exact location of a settlement.

Several physical factors were very important when locating early settlements:

- **Water supply** – a spring, river or well was needed.
- **Height** – above the flood plain a settlement is safe from flooding.
- **Defence** – a hill top or the inside of a river meander provided protection.
- **Shelter** – low lying land is more sheltered than uplands.
- **Soil** – fertile soils allowed farming of crops and animals.
- **Fuel** – wood was needed to burn for cooking and heat.
- **Building materials** – stone or wood was required to build houses.

Today many of these reasons for settlement location are outdated → political and economic reasons are more important.

Situation

Make sure you can explain the difference between site and situation.

If asked to give map evidence, use a grid reference.

Situation – the location of the settlement in relation to the surrounding area

– it is important in determining the success and growth of a settlement
– factors include access to other settlements and natural resources
– good transport links to other settlements should result in trade and growth.

Settlement patterns

Many settlements have a mixture of these patterns.

Settlement pattern – the **shape** and **distribution** of a settlement.

- **Dispersed** – isolated houses or farms → also found in areas of high relief.
- **Nucleated** – houses clustered together around a central point → a cross-roads, water supply or market place may be the focus.
- **Linear** – settlement built in a line → along a road or in a valley → sometimes called ribbon development.
- **Planned** – today many settlements are planned → different shapes exist: square, crescent and even aeroplane (Brasilia, Brazil).

Function

Settlements have several functions which will change over time.

Function – the social and economic activities of a settlement; settlements are sometimes described by a main function, e.g. Oxford – education.

Examples of functions

- **Residential** – providing housing is a main function of many settlements.
- **Administrative** – government and council offices.
- **Industrial** – includes heavy engineering and business parks.
- **Commercial** – shopping centres and retail parks.
- **Services** – schools and hospitals.

Settlement hierarchy

A pyramid represents this relationship.

Settlements may be arranged in rank order – a **hierarchy**; these can be shown using a pyramid. The order of importance is decided using three criteria:

- **Population size**
- **Services** – range and number
- **Distance apart**

– a **conurbation** is at the top of the hierarchy because it has a high population, a large range and number of services, and will be a long distance from other conurbations
– a **hamlet** is at the bottom because it has only a few people living there, possibly no services, and it is likely to be close to other hamlets
– as the rank of a settlement increases the fewer there will be of them → thousands of hamlets but only four or five conurbations.

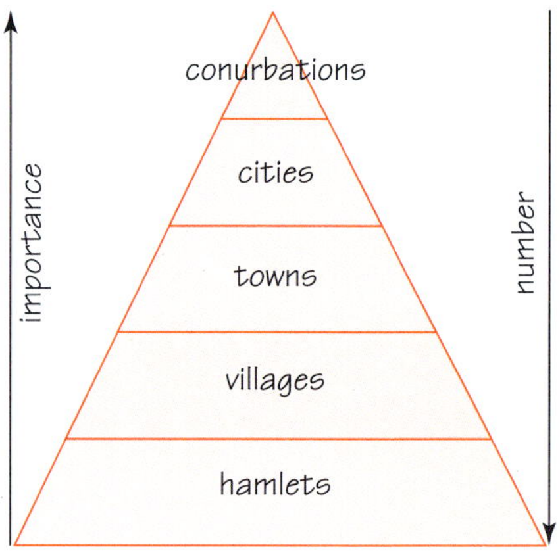

Range

Range, threshold and sphere of influence are important terms.

Range – is the **maximum distance** people are prepared to travel to use a service
– goods which are purchased frequently are called **convenience goods (low order)**
– convenience goods include newspapers and weekly shopping
– goods which are purchased infrequently are called **comparison goods (high order)**
– comparison goods are more expensive items such as televisions or furniture – people compare prices before deciding which shop to buy from
– people are prepared to travel greater distances for comparison goods – therefore as the hierarchy of a settlement increases so does its range.

Threshold

Threshold – the minimum number of people needed to support a service
– shop selling convenience goods needs a relatively low threshold population because people will buy things frequently
– shop selling comparison goods will require a larger population because people only buy these occasionally
– more specialist a shop or service – the larger the threshold population needed to support it
– settlement at the top of the hierarchy (high population) can support many services.

Sphere of influence

The **sphere of influence**, or **urban field** – the extent of a settlement's influence over the surrounding area.

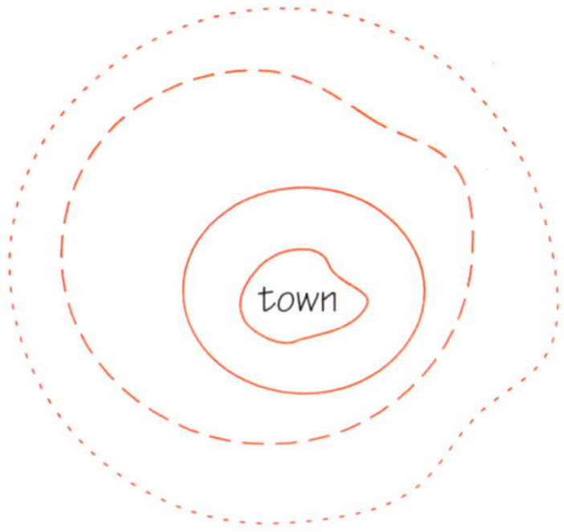

The sphere of influence of three services in a settlement.

newsagent
cinema
hospital

Urbanisation

Be clear about the difference between urbanisation and urban growth.

Urbanisation – increase in the percentage of people living in cities.
Urban growth – the expansion of towns and cities.
Both have occurred differently in MEDCs and LEDCs.

World-wide there are nearly 300 cities of over 1 million people – called 'million cities'.

Urbanisation in MEDCs

Began with the **Industrial Revolution** in the Nineteenth Century
- rural to urban migration occurred → migrants looking for work in factories
- houses were built around factories for workers → towns expanded to become cities
- today factories have been replaced by shops and offices at centre and 70% of population live in urban areas.

Urban land use models

Models – to identify and explain different types of land use in a city; they are an attempt to simplify reality – parts of all three may be found in a modern city.

Concentric circle model

- At the centre is the **Central Business District (CBD)** of shops and offices.
- Around the CBD is a '**twilight zone**' – an area in transition → old housing, abandoned industry and derelict land – part of the Inner City.
- Three housing zones follow – low, medium and high quality.

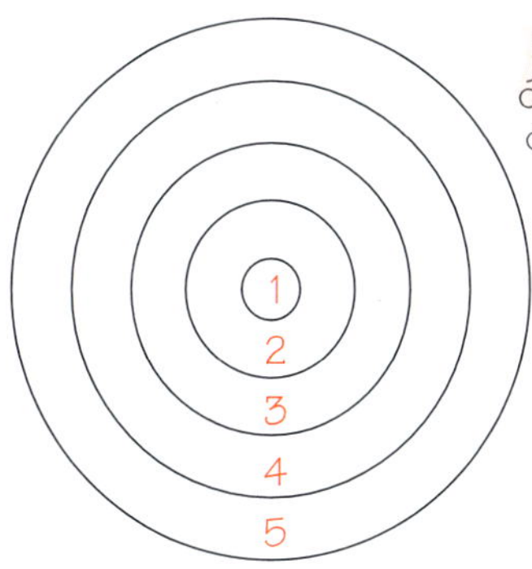

Land prices decrease with distance from the CBD.

Sector model

- Transport and physical factors are considered important in this model.
- As the city grew outwards, sectors of different land use developed along roads, railways and canals.

In reality land use in settlements is much more complex.

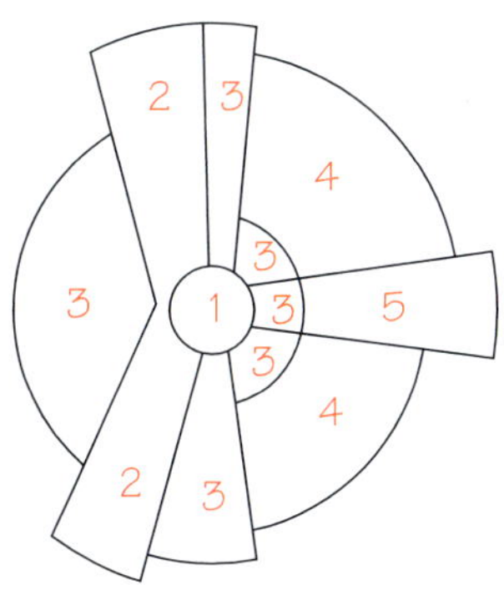

1 CBD
2 transition zone
3 low-cost housing
4 medium-cost housing
5 high-cost housing
6 industry

Multiple nuclei model

- A more realistic model which shows different land uses clustered together.
- Includes a greater variety of land use.

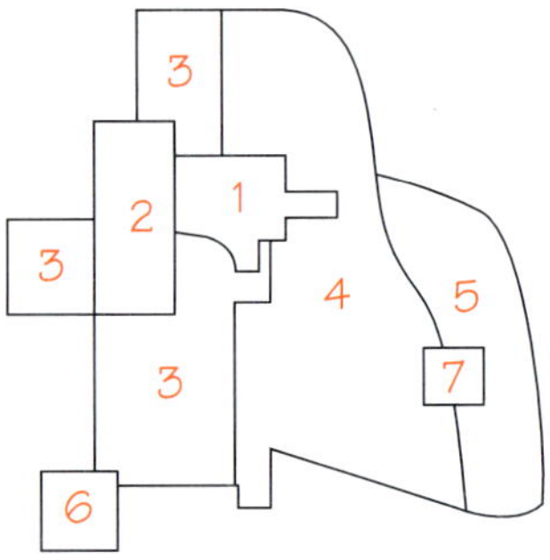

1 CBD
2 transition zone
3 low-cost housing
4 medium-cost housing
5 high-cost housing
6 industry
7 outlying business district

Urban change in the UK

Urban areas are constantly changing.

Exam questions frequently ask about change in urban areas.

- **Urban decay**
  - by the 1960s, inner city areas had become run-down and overcrowded
  - factories had closed due to poor access, changing technology and competition
  - high unemployment resulted → neighbourhoods declined → better-off moved out
  - housing was very poor → cramped, damp, shared bathrooms and no central heating.
- **Urban renewal**
  - **Redevelopment** – late 1960s, slum clearance took place → old terraced houses demolished; people were re-housed in new estates on outskirts and tower blocks in the inner city
  - problems with new estates → few services, expensive public transport, uneven social mix
  - problems with tower blocks → lacked sense of community, noisy, insecure, lower floors damp, stairwells threatening, lifts and central heating broke down
  - **Rehabilitation** – 1990s, inner city areas are being improved, rather than demolished and rebuilt – tenement flats converted to houses, derelict land turned into parks.

Be able to expand on urban renewal with examples.

- **Gentrification**
  - low quality housing in inner city is bought cheaply and improved by wealthy middle class
  - location offers good access to office jobs in CBD
  - encouraged by local authorities as it improves quality of area.

London Docklands has been gentrified.

- **Suburbanisation** – growth of residential areas and light industry at edge of city
  - new housing estates, business parks and out-of-town shopping centres are built.

Suburbanisation has contributed to the decline of the inner city.

- **Counter-urbanisation** – the migration of the better-off from urban to rural areas
  - happening in most MEDCs
  - caused by poor urban environments and the prospect of a better life in the countryside
  - commuting is possible due to improved transport – faster motorways and trains.
- **Green belts** – created in the 1950s when urban growth was threatening the countryside
  - areas of land around cities were protected from development
  - urban sprawl was contained as well as providing recreation areas for city dwellers.

In some cases Green Belts have been 'leap-frogged' and urban growth continued.

- **New towns** – first built in the 1950s – to prevent urban sprawl and regenerate declining areas
  - thirty three new towns have been built, relieving pressure from major cities
  - industries were attracted to new towns to provide employment.

Urbanisation in LEDCs

Urbanisation in LEDCs is happening faster than it did in MEDCs.

Urbanisation – increased since the 1950s – around 30% of people now live in urban areas
- rural-urban migration has increased the proportion of people living in cities
- poor harvests, lack of money and services have 'pushed' people from the countryside
- the possibility of paid employment, better education and healthcare have 'pulled' people to cities
- death rates have fallen due to improved healthcare → this has also led to a growth in the urban population
- cities in LEDCs are expanding outwards with little limit on growth.

Urban land use model

Exam questions may ask about differences between land use in a MEDC and a LEDC.

The model of a city in a LEDC is different from a MEDC
- at the centre is a CBD with shops, offices and some high quality housing – however it will be more congested and will contain traditional markets
- the quality of housing will decrease with distance from the CBD
- around the CBD will be high quality apartment blocks
- squatter settlements will develop on any derelict land or open spaces
- beyond this zone will be low quality permanent housing
- on the outskirts shanty towns/squatter settlements will have grown up
- industry will develop in zones along railways and roads.

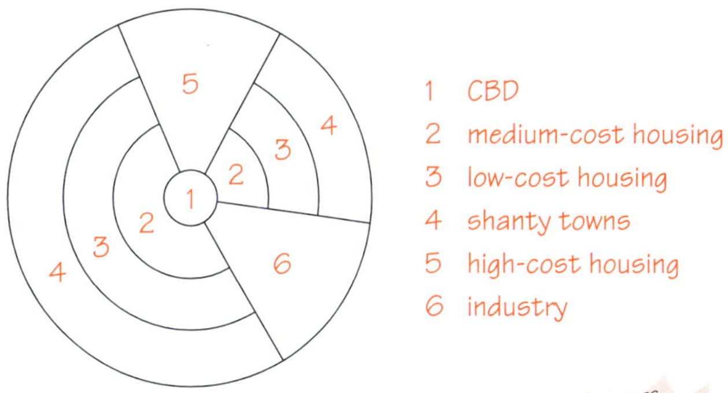

Squatter settlements

Squatter settlements are also called spontaneous settlements.

- squatter settlements develop as migrants arrive in the city
- shelters will be built from wood, cardboard, plastic and corrugated iron

Squatter settlements may be consolidated over time to form permanent medium quality housing.

Problems in squatter settlements

- **Population density will be high** → shelters will be very crowded.
- **Basic services are lacking** → no running water, no sewerage, no electricity, no waste disposal, no roads, no healthcare or schools.
- **Disease is common** → high infant mortality rate → short life expectancy.
- **Few formal jobs** → factories are too far away.
- **Location is often dangerous** → next to railway line or at risk of flooding.

An annotated sketch can be used to answer a question about housing improvements in LEDCs.

Solutions

- **Relocation** – build new apartment blocks for squatters → very expensive.
- **Self-help** – give squatters legal ownership of land → provide them with cheap materials to improve their homes → supply water, sewerage and electricity.
- **Site and service** – provide new plots of land with roads, and basic services → allow squatters to build own houses under guidance → can be very successful.

Settlement and urbanisation

Questions

1 What is the difference between 'site' and 'situation'?

2 What is meant by 'function'?

3 What type of settlement is at the top of a settlement hierarchy?

4 What is meant by 'range'?

5 What are 'comparison goods'?

6 Which will have a larger threshold – a newsagents or a supermarket?

7 What is the difference between 'urbanisation' and 'urban growth'?

8 What caused urbanisation in MEDCs?

9 What is urban decay?

10 What is the difference between urban 'redevelopment' and 'rehabilitation'?

11 How does 'gentrification' improve inner cities?

12 What is 'counter-urbanisation'?

13 Why were 'green belts' and 'new towns' created?

14 Why do people living in squatter settlements have poor access to services?

15 Why is disease common in squatter settlements?

Agriculture

Agriculture – using the land to grow crops and rear animals → farming.
Farming operates as a **system** with inputs, processes and outputs.

inputs	processes	outputs
climate, labour, relief, seeds, soil, animals	ploughing, harvesting, planting, grazing, weeding, milking	crops, animals, animal products

inputs → processes → outputs → profit → inputs

Be prepared to draw a systems diagram for different types of farming.

Factors affecting farming

The type of farming that is carried out depends on the interaction of a range of factors.

Seasonal distribution of precipitation is important – crops require regular watering during growth.

Physical factors

Climate varies with latitude.

- **Climate** – **temperature** – minimum of 6°C is needed for crops to grow
  - **length of growing season**, e.g. wheat requires 90 days
  - **precipitation** – at least 250 to 500 mm is required for crops.
- **Relief** – **altitude** – temperature decreases by 6.5 °C every 1000 metres – exposed to wind and rain
  - **aspect** – south facing slopes receive most sunshine (in Northern Hemisphere)
  - **angle of slope** – steep angle causes thin soils and limits use of machinery.

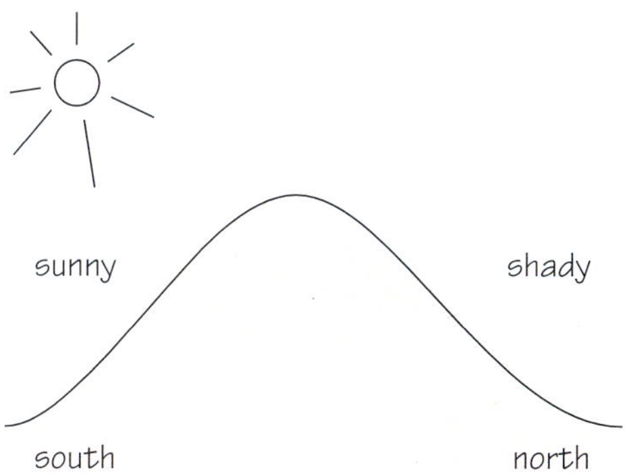

- **Soils** – **depth** – affects root growth
  - **nutrients** – released from weathered bedrock.
- **Drainage** – **impermeable bedrock** – may result in waterlogging
  - **permeable bedrock** – little surface drainage and thin soils.

Economic factors

- **Labour** – farming requires either **human labour** or **mechanisation**.
- **Market** – consumers tastes must be considered.
- **Accessibility** – **distance** and **time** to market
  - beyond a certain distance, transport costs exceed profits from sale of produce.

Political factors

Political factors are increasingly important.

- **Subsidies** – money is provided by governments to encourage certain agricultural practices.
- **Quotas** – governments place limits on production to prevent surpluses.

Behavioural factors

- **Perception factors** – **decisions** based on physical, economic and behavioural factors may be incorrect.
- **Attitudes** – **personal interests** will influence farmer's decisions.

Classification

Agriculture may be classified as contrasting systems. You must be able to **classify** different types of farming.

- **Arable or pastoral** – **arable** is the growing of crops
  - **pastoral** is the rearing of animals for meat and other products
  - **mixed** is a combination of the two.
- **Intensive or extensive** – **intensive** farming is a large input of money, labour or technology over a small area to produce high yields per hectare.
  - **extensive** farming is a small input of money, labour or technology over a large area to produce low yields per hectare.
- **Commercial or subsistence** – **commercial** farming produces crops or animals for sale and profit
  - **subsistence** farming produces food only for the farmer and family.
- **Nomadic or sedentary** – **nomadic** farming is shifting cultivation or seasonal movements of livestock for pasture
  - **sedentary** farming is established in one place.

Shifting cultivators remain in one place for many years.

Distribution of farming types in the UK

Physical, economic, political and behavioural factors combine to produce a distribution pattern of farming types in the UK.

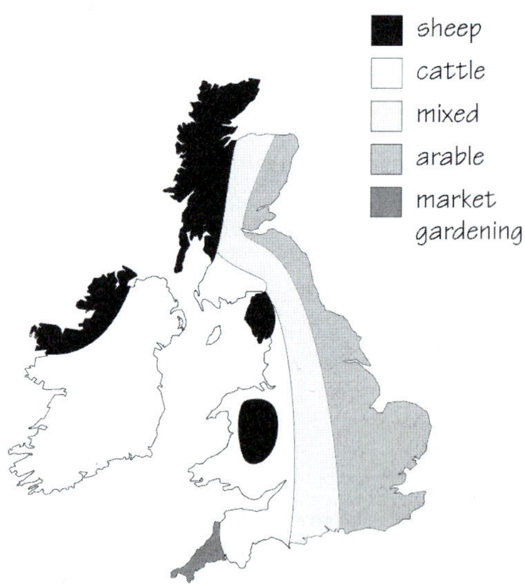

These locations are generalisations.

- **Dairy farming** – the rearing of cattle for milk and milk products
  - location – South-western parts of England, Scotland and Wales
  - flat relief, fertile well drained soils, high quality grass, mild winters and reliable rainfall
  - rapid access to large urban markets
  - subsidies for milk production after 1945
  - quotas introduced in the 1980s.
- **Arable farming** – the growing of cereal crops, vegetables and animal feeds
  - location – East and South-east of England
  - flat relief, deep rich soils, relatively dry, rain in growing season, warm summers and frost in winter to break up soil
  - minimum prices for arable products guaranteed by EU – **intervention**.
- **Sheep farming** – sheep are reared to provide meat and wool
  - location – upland areas in England, Wales and Scotland
  - high, steep relief, thin infertile soils, high rainfall and low temperatures
  - uneconomic to farm anything other than sheep
  - **subsidies** are provided for sheep farmers from the EU.
- **Market gardening** – very intensive farming of high value crops, such as fruit, vegetables and flowers – horticulture

- location – South-west England, Isles of Scilly and Fens
- hours of sunshine are important – most other physical factors are controlled
- glasshouses, heating, fertilisers, artificial soils and irrigation maximise growth
- produce is transported by aeroplane or refrigerated lorry to markets.

Common Agricultural Policy

Common Agricultural Policy (CAP) – agreed by the European Economic Community, now the European Union (EU), in 1962

These policies have encouraged farmers to use more intensive farming methods and to farm in more **marginal** areas.

Three aims:
- to protect the income of farmers
- to ensure reasonable and steady prices for consumers
- to provide sufficient food supplies by increasing production.

The CAP has achieved these aims through two main policies:
- **Grants and subsidies** – money provided for farmers in difficult areas, such as hill farms.
- **Intervention** – a guaranteed minimum price for agricultural produce → bought and stored by the EU, sold when price is favourable.

Environmental impacts of farming

Modern intensive farming methods have had an impact on the environment.

Modern farming methods have allowed cheap high quality food to be produced.

- **Hedgerows** – have been removed to allow easier access for farm machinery
  - wildlife has been greatly affected – hedgerows act as wildlife corridors.
- **Soil erosion** – ploughed land on steep slopes increases run-off and soil erosion
  - fertilisers have reduced soil humus – more easily blown away.
- **Fertilisers** – overuse means **nitrates** washed into rivers → causes **algae** to grow → removes **oxygen** → kills river-life → this is called **eutrophication**
  - water supply can be contaminated with nitrates.
- **Pesticides and herbicides** – kill insects, weeds and fungi → also damage beneficial organisms
  - **leaching** and run-off deposits pesticides in rivers → enters food chain → kills wildlife.

Farm diversification

Diversification – a move into other areas of business.
Food surpluses, quotas, reduced subsidies and a growing environmental awareness has led to many farms diversifying.

The high cost of new machinery has encouraged farmers to diversify.

- **PYO** – Pick Your Own schemes are marketed to the public as a leisure activity whilst reducing labour costs for the farmer.
- **Farm and garden centres** – sale of farm produce and gardening-based products.
- **Organic farming** – cultivation without artificial fertilisers or pesticides.
- **B&B** – barns are converted into holiday cottages.

Set-aside

Problem is that farmers may take least fertile land out of production → does not have full impact on reducing surpluses.

- **Set-aside** – an EU funded scheme to reduce surpluses
  - farmers are paid not to cultivate up to 18% of their land, for five years
  - land may be left **fallow**, planted with trees or used for non-agricultural use
  - payment is £250, per hectare, per year.

Farming in LEDCs

Population growth in LEDCs has led to an increased demand for food production – high-technology farming methods were introduced in the 1960s and 1970s – food production has risen dramatically, but with some problems – today, intermediate technology farming methods are considered more appropriate for many poorer countries.

Green revolution

The green revolution was concentrated in Asia and South America.

Green revolution – the increase in agricultural output caused by the introduction of capital intensive farming methods in LEDCs.

- **High Yield Variety crops** – HYV crops of rice and wheat are faster growing and give an increase in yield.
- **Fertilisers** – artificial fertilisers are used to feed HYV crops.
- **Herbicides** – weeds are controlled with chemicals.
- **Pesticides** – insects are killed with poisonous sprays.
- **Irrigation** – HYV crops require more water than traditional varieties.
- **Machinery** – farm processes mechanised → buffalo replaced by tractors.

Biotechnology is continuing the green revolution with genetically altered crops such as soyabeans.

Successes

- **yields** have increased up to three times
- output has risen → countries now export grain rather than import it
- HYV crops grow quickly → allows two crops to be grown each year
- additional vegetable crops can be grown
- standard of living for some farmers has risen.

Problems

- benefits of green revolution were concentrated on better-off land owners who could afford new inputs
- landless labourers were evicted to make way for new technology
- mechanisation has increased unemployment
- gap between rich and poor has grown
- HYV crops require irrigation → not always available
- fertilisers and pesticides must be purchased from chemical companies in MEDCs
- HYV seeds must be purchased every year → seeds from crop are **infertile**
- chemicals are dangerous to health if used incorrectly
- **monoculture** (one breed of crop) carries a greater risk of disease
- much of the increase in production is exported → poor cannot afford to buy it.

Intermediate technology

It is recognised that the green revolution has not benefited people equally; **intermediate technology** aims to increase food production in ways more appropriate to LEDCs.

- **Water supply** – wells, pumps and drip irrigation provide a cheap and effective means of providing water for crops.
- **Soil erosion** – planting trees as windbreaks and building stone lines on contours (restricts run-off) reduces the amount of soil lost.
- **Soil fertility** – **leguminous crops** fix nitrogen in the soil, increasing soil fertility.
- **Intercropping** – crops may be grown at different levels to maximise productivity → trees, plants and root vegetables.
- **Food storage** – well designed grain stores prevent losses from rats and insects.

Agriculture Questions

1 Classify the following as farming inputs, processes or outputs: Crops, Weeding, Profit, Soil, Grazing, Climate.

2 What is meant by growing season?

3 How does altitude affect farming?

4 How does bedrock influence farming?

5 What is a 'quota'?

6 What is the difference between 'subsistence' and 'commercial' farming?

7 What is the CAP?

8 What is 'intervention'?

9 Why have hedgerows been removed from fields?

10 What is farm 'diversification'?

11 What is the 'green revolution'?

12 What is irrigation?

13 Who has benefited most from the green revolution?

14 Why does using HYV crops make farmers dependent on companies in MEDCs?

15 The green revolution has resulted in large increases in yields – why are millions in LEDCs still undernourished?

Industry

Industry – any type of economic activity, or employment, producing goods or providing services
– includes agriculture, manufacturing and service industries
– usually exists with the aim of making a profit, or providing a public service
– varies in nature over time and between different countries.

Classification

Quaternay and tertiary are often combined for statistics.

Industry is divided into four sectors:

- **Primary industry** – extraction or production of **raw materials** → includes agriculture, forestry, fishing and mining.
- **Secondary industry** – **processing** of raw materials, or **assembling** components to make a finished product → includes steel making and car assembly.
- **Tertiary industry** – provision of **services** such as health, administration, retailing and transport → also called 'service industries'.
- **Quaternary industry** – provision of advice or **information**, or **research** → includes financial advisers, research scientists and education.

Industry may also be classified as capital or labour intensive:

- **Capital intensive** – industries requiring a large investment in buildings, machinery and technology → usually found in MEDCs.
- **Labour intensive** – industries requiring a large labour force, rather than machinery → associated with LEDCs.

Industry as a system

Industry operates as a system with inputs, processes and outputs.

Be prepared to draw a systems diagram for various industries.

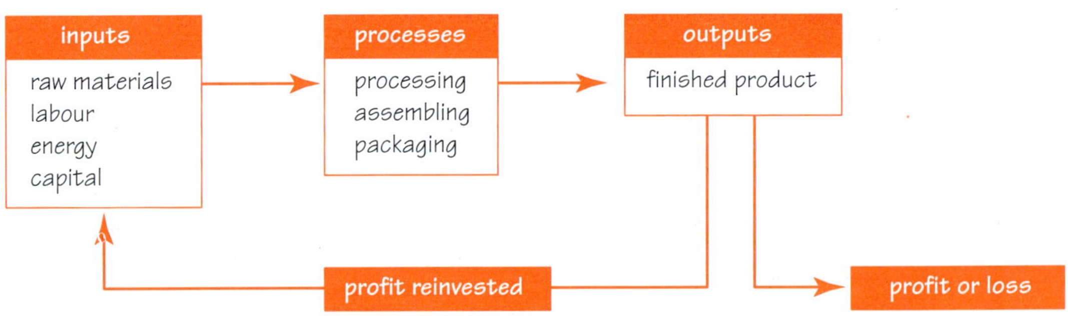

– the finished product is sold and the money earned is re-invested in the industry to buy more raw materials, pay wages and bills and repay loans
– **profit** is the money left after re-investment → paid to shareholders in a large company.

Occupational structures

The term '**occupational**' is more accurate than '**employment**' because in many countries agricultural workers are not employed, but work to provide food for their family.

Occupational (employment) structures – describe the percentage of workers involved in primary, secondary and tertiary industry in an area

– shown as either a **pie chart** or a **triangular graph**

Make sure you can interpret and complete pie charts and triangular graphs.

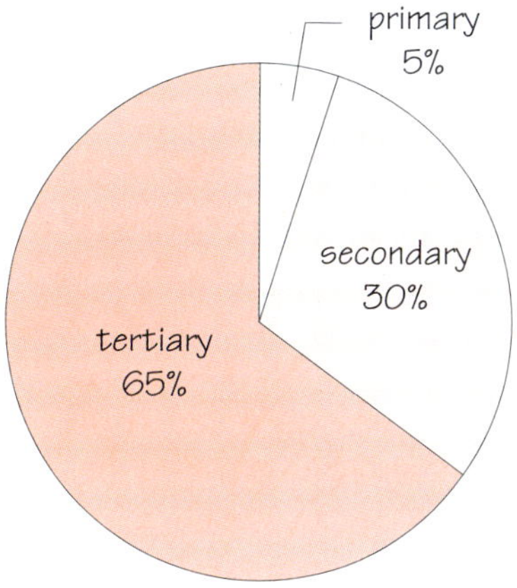

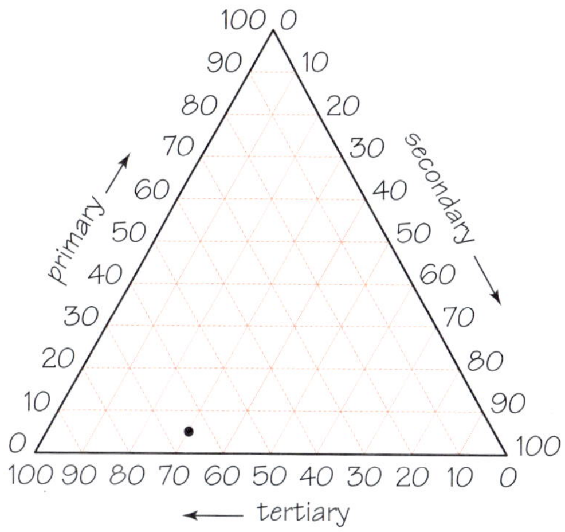

– occupational structures change over time as a country experiences industrialisation and de-industrialisation

– **industrialisation** is the development of a manufacturing-based society, having been dependent on agriculture

– **de-industrialisation** is the move away from manufacturing to a society based on service industries

– LEDCs have a high percentage or workers in primary industry

– MEDCs have the majority of workers employed in tertiary industry.

Location of industry

Different types of industry have different location needs.

The decision about where to locate an industry is based on several factors:

- **Raw materials** – distance from raw materials is important for manufacturing industries if they have to transport heavy and bulky goods.
- **Market** – a population to purchase the goods or services needs to be accessible.
- **Labour** – a workforce is needed → cost and skill level of workers will be considered.
- **Energy** – originally industries tied to coal deposits → today electricity allows more freedom.
- **Site** – factories require large areas of flat land, especially if using an assembly line.
- **Communications** – good road, rail, sea and air transport networks are required for the import and export of goods – reliable telecommunications are increasingly important.
- **Capital** – money is needed to invest in buildings and machinery → obtained from shareholders and bank loans.
- **Government policy** – development is restricted in some areas and encouraged in others with the use of incentives such as grants, rent free buildings and tax concessions.
- **Industrial inertia** – industries remain concentrated in an area although the factors responsible for their original location are no longer important.
- **Environment** – an attractive environment with good leisure facilities is increasingly important in attracting a workforce.

Changing nature of manufacturing industry

- **Heavy industry** – the manufacture of goods which require large amounts of bulky raw materials, e.g. iron and steel making
  - locates near to a source of raw materials
  - in decline in importance in MEDCs due to exhaustion of raw materials, markets no longer available, competition from other countries, failure to invest in new technology.

Raw material orientated industry.

- **Light industry** – the production of high value goods, e.g. car stereos
  - locates within reach of a market
  - becomes increasingly important as a country develops economically.

Market orientated industry.

- **Hi-tech industry** – the production of very high value goods, e.g. computing, biotechnology, and telecommunications
  - most important location factor is the workforce
  - research and development is concentrated in MEDCs → highly educated workforce
  - **assembly** is located in LEDCs where semi-skilled workers' wages are lower
  - often described as 'foot loose' because they are not tied to a particular location by raw materials and markets.

Footloose industry.

Science and business parks

Greenfield sites are attractive countryside locations, often on city outskirts.

Many light and hi-tech industries locate in **business** or **science parks**, on **greenfield sites**
- **business parks** are planned developments of offices, and light and hi-tech industry – often in areas suffering from decline of heavy industry
- **science parks** are hi-tech industrial developments located close to universities
- universities provide a highly skilled workforce
- businesses provide sponsorship for university research.

Development Areas

Development areas attract overseas investment.

Areas suffering from decline of traditional heavy industries have high unemployment – governments attempt to regenerate an area by naming it a **Development Area** with special status to encourage new industries to locate there
- grants are awarded to companies who establish new factories
- ready-built premises with low rents are provided
- communications are improved for good accessibility
- advertising promotes the advantages of the area
- **Enterprise Zones** have the benefits of reduced taxes and relaxed planning laws, for ten years
- **Urban Development Corporations** reclaim derelict land and prepare new sites for industry.

The multiplier operates in reverse if a large employer in an area closes down.

Multiplier effect

Use this term when explaining impact of industrial growth or decline.

Multiplier effect – the economic impact of industrial development on an area
- new industry locates in area → other industries required to supply **components** and **services** → jobs are created → workers have more **disposable income** → local businesses benefit → area increases in prosperity → new industries are attracted.

ɔwn as **retailing**; traditionally they have located in
ssible – since the 1980s, the UK retail industry has
ɔan areas.

– several types:
rket, or hypermarket – frequently with a petrol

ıch as garden centres, furniture, carpet, toy and DIY

ın undercover shopping mall, containing two or three
further shops, restaurants, cinemas and huge car

ilt shopping centre where chain stores sell

:ion

has followed the movement of people from cities to
the suburbs.

- **Car ownership** – a more mobile population as car ownership has increased.
- **Motorways** – improved road network has reduced travel times.
- **Parking** – parking is easy and free at out of town shopping centres.
- **Government policy** – planning permission encouraged development.

Government policy is now to restrict development of out of town shopping centres.

Conflicts

The growth of out of town shopping centres has created **conflicts**:
- town and city centres have lost many **chain stores** as they relocated
- independent shops have lost trade and had to close down
- vacant premises are filled by charity and discount shops
- town centre becomes run-down and unattractive
- out of town locations are not easily accessible for elderly and poor without cars
- **Urban sprawl** is encouraged by development on **greenfield sites**.

International trade

International trade – the exchange of goods and services between countries
- '**balance of trade**' is the difference between money earned from exports and money spent on imports
- both MEDCs and LEDCs will have a '**trade deficit**', if they import more than they export
- **invisible imports** and **exports** occur when services are bought or sold → no physical movement of goods takes place
- the global pattern of trade is for MEDCs to export mainly manufactured goods or services and LEDCs to export mainly primary products
- currently 75% of world manufacturing happens in MEDCs → this pattern is changing as many LEDCs industrialise.

For more detail see 'Development and interdependence' chapter.

Transnational Corporations

> The turnover of a large TNC is larger than the GNP of many LEDCs.

Transnational Corporations (TNCs), or multinationals – very large companies with offices and factories all over the world e.g. Ford, IBM, Exxon
– globally, employ millions of people.

TNCs locate in many different countries for several reasons:
– access is gained to **potential markets**
– **trade barriers**, such as **tariffs** and **quotas**, can be avoided
– **low labour costs** in LEDCs allow increased profit
– **governments** encourage TNCs to locate in their country
– **communications** have improved – satellite phones, E-mail, internet and video conferencing
– **headquarters** and **research and development** offices are usually located in MEDCs
– **factories** are located all over the world, but particularly in LEDCs.

> A common exam question asks about the advantages and disadvantages of TNCs.

Advantages of TNCs

– employment is provided, increasing prosperity of area
– taxes are paid to the government
– technology and skills are transferred between countries
– **infrastructure** and services may be improved.

Disadvantages of TNCs

– TNCs may use their power to influence governments
– profit is transferred to TNC headquarters, usually in MEDCs
– many jobs are low-skill assembly
– wages are low and working conditions sometimes poor
– TNCs' activities may cause environmental damage.

Industry in LEDCs

Industrialisation in LEDCs – seen by many as the key to economic development; however, there are several barriers to industrialisation:
– capital for investment is limited
– transport networks are poor and affected by weather
– electricity is unreliable or not available
– lack of skilled labour and management expertise
– local markets are limited
– corrupt government officials
– unfair trading practices of MEDCs.

> Appropriate technology, which is low-tech and labour intensive, may be more suitable for LEDCs.

Newly Industrialised Countries

Newly Industrialised Countries (NICs) – were previously LEDCs – have developed an economy based on manufacturing since the 1960s
– examples include Singapore, Hong Kong, South Korea and Brazil.

Strategies

Governments of NICs have used a number of strategies to achieve industrial development:

Many NICs suffered economic problems in 1998 due to high cost of debt repayments.

- **cheap loans** and **subsidies** were given to new industries
- **imports** were **restricted** to protect own industries from competition
- **currencies** were **devalued** to make exports cheaper
- **tax holidays** were offered to overseas investors → no tax to pay for several years
- **Free Trade Zones** established → no customs duties
- **Trade union activity** and strikes were banned
- **Health** and **safety regulations** in factories were not enforced
- **education** and **training** was prioritised to attract high-tech TNCs.

Successes

- manufacturing industry has progressed from textiles and clothes to high-tech electronics
- wages and living standards have risen
- industries have grown in TNCs and are now expanding globally.

Problems

- tax holidays finish → TNCs close factories and re-locate in other countries
- skill levels and wages rise → workers in other LEDCs become cheaper
- NICs have borrowed heavily → if growth slows they face huge economic problems.

Environmental impact of industry

Industrialisation is beneficial economically – however, it has an impact on the environment.

See 'Global environmental problems' chapter.

As LEDCs develop economically, environmental damage will increase.

- **Air**
  - **global warming** – caused by polluting gases from power stations and factories
  - **acid deposition** – pollutants from power stations damage lakes and trees
  - **ozone layer damage** – CFC gases used in industry are damaging the ozone layer.

- **Land** – extractive industries scar the landscape and produce spoil tips of waste materials
  - industrial waste is dumped in landfill sites
  - toxic material poisons land, people and wildlife.

- **Noise and view** – people living close to factories or mines will suffer visual and noise pollution.

- **Water**
  - power stations use river water for cooling → returned warm with lower oxygen content → harms river life
  - toxic chemicals are discharged by factories into rivers → heavy metals (mercury, lead, zinc) build up in fish → unfit for human consumption → fish become deformed
  - chemicals are reducing fertility of river creatures
  - domestic water supply may become contaminated
  - accidental spillages of chemicals or oil from ships occur
  - rivers discharge into seas → main cause of sea pollution.

Industry

Questions

1 What are the four sectors of industry?

2 What is an 'occupational structure'?

3 Why do occupational structures change over time?

4 What is 'de-industrialisation'?

5 Why is energy no longer such an important location factor?

6 What is 'industrial inertia'?

7 What is the most important location factor for heavy industry?

8 Why is hi-tech industry described as footloose?

9 What benefits does an 'Enterprise Zone' give to industry?

10 What is the 'balance of trade'?

11 What is a TNC?

12 How do communications restrict industrialisation in LEDCs?

13 What is a 'NIC'?

14 Why are tax holidays not always a long-term strategy?

15 How do power stations pollute rivers?

Leisure and tourism

Leisure

Leisure-time – considered to be free-time – time available after work, housework and sleep
- leisure has grown in importance this century, as an activity and as an industry
- people now spend, on average, 30% of their disposable income on leisure activities
- leisure activities have both benefits and disadvantages.

Recreation

Recreation is an activity undertaken during leisure time – lasting less than 24 hours.
- **Recreation** may be entertaining, amusing, improving a skill or just rest and relaxation.
- **Active recreation** – a person is physically involved, e.g. sport.
- **Passive recreation** – observing only, e.g. watching the TV.
- **Formal recreation** – an organised activity, e.g. aerobics.
- **Informal recreation** – less organised, fewer participants, e.g. a walk in the park.

Tourism

Tourism – another way of spending leisure time – visiting places and usually spending at least one night away from home → a **holiday**.

Growth in recreation and tourism

A common focus of exam questions.

Mass tourism – today there are 700 million international tourist visits worldwide every year.

The huge growth in tourism has been caused by several changes since the 1950s:
- **Paid holiday** – increase in number of weeks paid annual leave.
- **Shorter working week** – UK 1970s average 45 hours – 1990s average, 38 hours.
- **Wages** – pay has increased faster than inflation → people better off.
- **Attitudes** – people now expect to have a summer holiday.
- **Adventure** – life has become safer → people want excitement.
- **Television** – increase in number of travel programmes, e.g. 'Wish you were here'.
- **Elderly** – early retirement and increased life expectancy → growth in activities for over 60s.
- **Cars** – more people own cars and motorway networks have improved.
- **Air fares** – charter airlines and independent travel agents offer cheap flights.

Environment

When describing the attractions of a tourist destination consider these factors.

Tourism will only develop in an area if it has an attractive environment – influencing factors include:
- **Climate** – summer holidays → warm to hot temperatures → low humidity → little and infrequent rain; winter holidays → skiing destinations will require cold temperatures and plenty of snow.
- **Scenery** – interesting relief and features such as mountains, hills, valleys, rivers, waterfalls, cliffs, beaches and caves.
- **Ecology** – a variety of trees and plants – interesting animals, birds and marine life.
- **Culture** – a place with an interesting history, impressive architecture, museums, distinctive food, traditional music or an exciting nightlife.
- **Activities** – destinations offering activities such as wind-surfing, water-skiing, mountain biking, walking, horse-riding, etc.

Changing destinations

Package holidays include flights, accommodation, food and the services of a holiday rep.

Tourism in the UK began during the last century
- seaside towns such as Blackpool and Brighton developed as holiday destinations
- unreliable British weather often caused disappointment
- In the 1970s, **package holidays** to Europe became popular
- cheap package deals and guaranteed good weather led to decline of UK resorts
- attractive Mediterranean coastal villages developed → hotels, bars and nightclubs built
- by the 1980s many resorts were over developed → original charm and culture gone → replaced by English style pubs and fish and chip shops
- many Mediterranean resorts declined in popularity
- **long haul** holiday destinations have become popular in the 1990s → areas outside Europe, such as Florida, Barbados, Kenya and Thailand.

New and unspoilt tourist destinations are continually in demand worldwide.

Types of holiday

Today, in addition to package holidays, a variety of tourism options are available:
- **Weekend-break** – a reduced price stay in a business hotel, or a city break in a European city.
- **Family holiday** – designed with children in mind → organised activities based in a resort complex → baby-sitting and evening entertainment.
- **18 to 30 holiday** – limited to people between 18 and 30 → organised activities and a wild nightlife.
- **Self-catering** – an apartment or house which allows people to cook own meals.
- **Fly-drive** – a flight and a rental car at the destination → hotels may not be pre-booked.
- **Independent** – backpackers on a low budget – long term travellers, possibly with a 'round-the-world' air ticket.

Tourism as an export

An important concept – 'invisible export'.

Tourism may be described as an '**export**' since it is an important source of income for a country
- the UK earns £38 billion a year from around 24 million tourists
- LEDCs see income from tourism as a way to break out of the poverty trap
- income from tourism will depend on currency exchange rates and competition from other resorts.

Seasonality

- **Seasonality** – how tourism is affected by different times of the year
  - coastal resorts are busiest in the summer
  - ski resorts are busiest in the winter
  - all resorts may be affected by the timing of school holidays.
- **Seasonality causes problems for tourist destinations**
  - crowds in high season may place strain on the infrastructure → water supply, roads, etc
  - during the low season many workers will become unemployed.
- **Resorts will attempt to extend their tourist season to maximise profit**
  - Blackpool uses the illuminations in Autumn to attract visitors
  - ski resorts market themselves as areas for walking holidays in the summer
  - Mediterranean resorts attract the over 50s with cheap long-term winter holidays
  - resorts in MEDCs may attempt to make their attractions 'weather-proof', e.g. Center Parcs.

National Parks

National Parks are large areas of attractive countryside which are protected by law
– idea began in the USA last century
– found today in over 100 countries.

National Parks in England and Wales

In the USA, National Parks are wilderness areas, in England and Wales they are working areas.

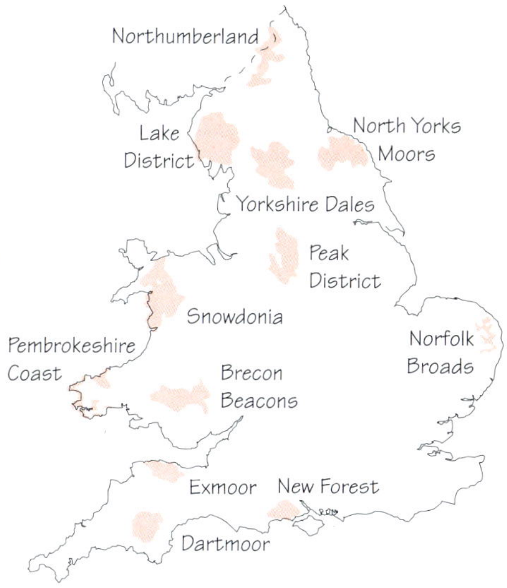

- **Aims** – stated in the 1949 National Parks and Access to the Countryside Act
  – the beauty of the landscape is preserved
  – public are given access to enjoy recreation
  – wildlife and important buildings are preserved
  – traditional farming methods are continued.
- **Status** – the largest landowners are the National Trust, Forestry Commission and Ministry of Defence.
- **Characteristics** – usually areas of beautiful **upland scenery** – containing mountains, hills, moors, lakes, forests or coastline
  – the Peak District was the first National Park – established 1949
  – ten National Parks now exist, with the Norfolk Broads and the New Forest given the same level of protection
  – include recreation opportunities e.g. walking, cycling, climbing, camping, watersports, etc
  – administered by a **National Park Authority (NPA)** → however, 98% of the land in the National Parks is privately owned
  – National Parks are working areas – agriculture, forestry and quarrying take place.

Conflicts

The growth of the leisure industry has benefited people living in National Parks by providing employment and bringing money into the area – however, conflicts arise between tourists, locals, farmers and industry.

1000 boats are registered for use on Lake Windermere, Lake District.

Honeypots may be developed deliberately to relieve pressure on more sensitive areas.

- **Traffic congestion** – too many cars on narrow roads, and poor parking damages verges.
- **Soil erosion** – footpaths are being worn away by huge numbers of walkers.
- **Honeypots** – areas that attract most visitors are called 'honeypots' – development at honeypots is destroying features that made them popular in the first place.
- **Holiday cottages** – purchase of homes as holiday cottages has increased prices and made it more difficult for local people to continue living in area.
- **Quarrying** – quarries provide local jobs but scar the landscape.

Management

National Parks are under pressure from the huge numbers of environmentally aware visitors, rather than the few who may drop litter or leave gates open.

NPAs must try to **conserve** the environment and **minimise conflicts** – methods include:
– reduce traffic and parking problems with park and ride schemes
– reinforce footpaths and plan new routes
– either 'sacrifice' honeypot sites for sake of other areas, or develop other sites
– allow new homes to be built → targeted at young locals
– ensure any quarries are fully landscaped and restored after use.

Tourism in less economically developed countries

Tourism in LEDCs accounts for only 20% of holidays taken – however, this percentage is growing every year – countries such as Kenya, Thailand, Mexico, Egypt and China have well established tourist industries.

- **Reasons for growth**
  - government investment – spending on international airports, roads and hotels
  - advertising – promotion of country overseas through magazine adverts and tourist offices
  - LEDC countries are very cheap for visitors from MEDCs
  - Mediterranean sites have become **over-developed**
  - visitors want to experience something more **exotic** → broaden their horizons
  - reliable **good weather** all year round
  - long-haul flights have fallen in price and new planes are able to fly direct.

Exam questions often ask about the benefits and disadvantages of tourism in LEDCs.

- **Benefits**
  - income from tourism is invested in industry in an attempt to break out of a **cycle of underdevelopment**
  - schools and hospitals may benefit from increased revenue
  - hotels provide a market for farmers' products
  - employment is created – making and selling souvenirs, taxi drivers, guides and hotel jobs
  - a country's infrastructure may be improved.

If an area becomes over-developed people are no longer keen to visit – a balance must be obtained.

- **Disadvantages**

  Uncontrolled tourism may create many problems in LEDCs:
  - building of hotels uses up land and can make an area unattractive
  - hotels built on the beach will displace fishermen
  - many hotels are owned by international companies → profits leave the country
  - food and drink may be imported to suit tourist tastes
  - local culture may be lost, or turned into a nightly show for tourists
  - social problems of crime, prostitution and drug use are introduced
  - tourists may display a lack of respect for local customs and religion
  - hotels demand valuable water resources for swimming pools and showers
  - tourist activities may cause environmental damage to ecosystems.

Eco-tourism includes activities such as whale watching – exploiting wildlife without harming it.

- **Sustainable tourism**

  Some LEDCs have learned from the 'boom and bust' of other world resorts and are promoting **sustainable** tourism – mass tourism is avoided – instead small groups of wealthy **eco-tourists** are encouraged
  - the environment is protected by limiting development
  - hotels are allowed to be built at a height of only one storey
  - resorts are landscaped to fit in with the environment
  - tourist development is integrated into local towns, rather than building separate complexes
  - tourist police units established → to protect and inform visitors
  - tourists are educated about local culture and customs
  - taxes are charged → money used to benefit local area.

Leisure and tourism

Questions

1 What is recreation?

2 How have changes in working conditions led to 'mass tourism'?

3 Why has there been a growth in demand for leisure activities for the elderly?

4 What is a 'package holiday'?

5 What is a 'long-haul' destination?

6 Why is tourism described as an export?

7 What is 'seasonality'?

8 What problems are faced by resorts during the low season?

9 What is a National Park?

10 How many National Parks are there in England and Wales?

11 How has tourism benefited National Parks?

12 What is a 'honey-pot'?

13 How can the pressure on 'honey-pots' be reduced?

14 How have governments of LEDCs encouraged tourism?

15 What is meant by 'sustainable-tourism'?

Energy

Energy and fuel

The sun is the source of all energy – apart from geothermal.

Energy – the power needed to run machines and provide heat and light – essential for human life.

Fuel – a store of energy.

Globally there is an increase in the demand for energy due to **population growth** and **economic development** – expected increase of 50% by 2020.

Resources and consumption

Fuel resources and demand for energy are not evenly **distributed** around the world

- MEDCs contain only 25% of the world's population, however they consume 80% of the total energy produced
- LEDCs rarely have any significant reserves of fuel, when they do, they often export it to MEDCs
- in some MEDCs, the demand for energy is slowly decreasing due to more efficient cars and household appliances
- in LEDCs the demand for energy is set to rise dramatically → in China (population 1.3 billion) most families do not yet own a car.

The average American uses 35 times more energy than the average Indian.

Non-renewable and renewable energy

MEDCs use **secondary** energy – electricity distributed by cable; LEDCs use primary energy-fuel, e.g. wood and animal dung.

Energy sources are divided into two categories – **non-renewable and renewable**

- **Non-renewable** – coal, oil and gas → also known as fossil fuels as they were formed millions of years ago – they are finite → once they have been used they cannot be replaced.
- Nuclear power is also non-renewable – **Uranium**, the raw material, is a finite resource – however current reserves will last for over 1000 years.
- **Renewable sources** – hydro-electric power (HEP), solar, wind, geothermal, wave and tidal power – all are **inexhaustible** – can be used for ever.
- **Fuelwood** is, in theory, renewable – in practice trees are cut down faster than they are replaced – in which case they become a non-renewable resource.

Non-renewable energy sources

In total about 95% of the world's energy comes from non-renewable sources.

Coal

Coal was formed 300 million years ago.

Coal – **sedimentary rock** with a high carbon content formed from compressed remains of trees and plants; used as a **primary fuel** in homes; burned to provide electricity in power stations

- large coal deposits are found in the USA, Western Europe, South Africa and India
- it is mined either underground or by open-cast mining
- competition from oil and gas and cheaper imported coal has led to closure of many UK mines – has resulted in **high unemployment** and **deprivation** in mining towns → knock on effect for local businesses.

Multiplier effect.

Advantages – coal still has large reserves, about 300 years worth – it is a relatively efficient source of energy.

Disadvantages – open cast mines create visual, noise and air pollution – underground mines may collapse killing miners – gas explosions – large **spoil heaps** are produced – coal is bulky to transport – gases produced by burning coal cause **global warming** and **acid rain**.

Oil and gas

Oil and gas were formed 200 million years ago.

Oil and **gas** are formed from the remains of tiny sea creatures that died millions of years ago – they are found together trapped in **pockets** beneath layers of **impermeable rock**

- both are burned to provide electricity as well as being used domestically
- major oil and gas fields are found in the Persian Gulf, Alaska and the North Sea
- oil and gas are brought to the surface by drilling wells – both will gush out under pressure → later will need to be pumped out
- drilling for oil can be challenging – frozen ground in Alaska makes drilling difficult
- massive oil rigs have been designed to drill for oil at sea – danger of explosion and fire.

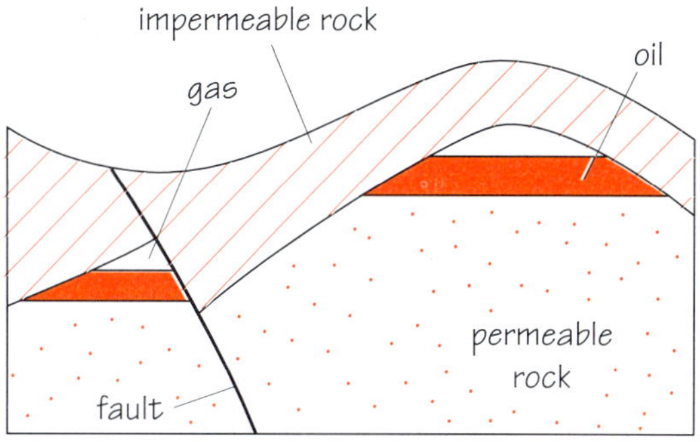

Oil is a vital raw material used to make products such as petrol and plastic.

Advantages – oil and gas are easy to transport, both by pipeline, oil by tanker – cheaper and cleaner than coal, less than half the amount of greenhouse gases – gas and oil fired power stations are less visually intrusive.

Disadvantages – oil reserves may be used up by 2035, gas reserves by 2050 – risk of serious environmental damage if pipeline breaks or tanker is grounded, e.g. Exxon Valdez 1989 – oil should not be wasted as it is such an important raw material for other products – major reserves are in areas of political instability, e.g. Iraq.

Nuclear

Nuclear energy is provided by **uranium** – a radioactive mineral

- uranium atoms are split by nuclear **fission** → creates great heat → produces steam → steam drives turbine → generates electricity
- refined uranium is easy to transport → power stations not tied to site of raw material, however do need huge quantities of water for cooling → majority are located on coast
- public concerns over the safety of nuclear power have caused governments to look for alternatives where available.

People have strong opinions about nuclear power.

Advantages – uranium reserves will last for many years – power stations produce no greenhouse gases – countries with no fossil fuel reserves are less dependent on other countries.

Disadvantages – risk of radiation leak or reactor meltdown, fallout carried many miles by wind – causes cancer, e.g. Chernobyl in Ukraine, 1986 – nuclear waste remains radioactive for hundreds of years – plans to bury it deep underground, however environmental groups say this is not safe – **decommissioning** (closing) of old nuclear power stations is incredibly expensive – makes long term cost high.

Fuelwood

Fuelwood is a primary fuel.

Collecting firewood is very time consuming – may contribute to under-development.

In many areas of LEDCs, electricity is either not available or unreliable;

fuelwood is the most important source of energy
- particularly in the countryside people must either collect fuelwood themselves, or buy it, to burn at home for heating and cooking
- **intermediate technology** solutions are helping to solve problem – a more efficient cooking stove has been introduced in Kenya which uses less wood.

Advantages – it is a low technology source of energy, less to go wrong – LEDCs do not have to spend money on importing expensive fossil fuels.

Disadvantages – increase in demand means that live trees are cut for fuel → they are rarely replanted, supplies are running out → may increase desertification.

Renewable energy sources

Presently most renewable energy sources are **uneconomic** compared to fossil fuels.

Extracting and burning fossil fuels harms the environment; fossil fuels will also run out in the future; other, permanent, less polluting, forms of energy have been developed.

Hydro-electric power (HEP)

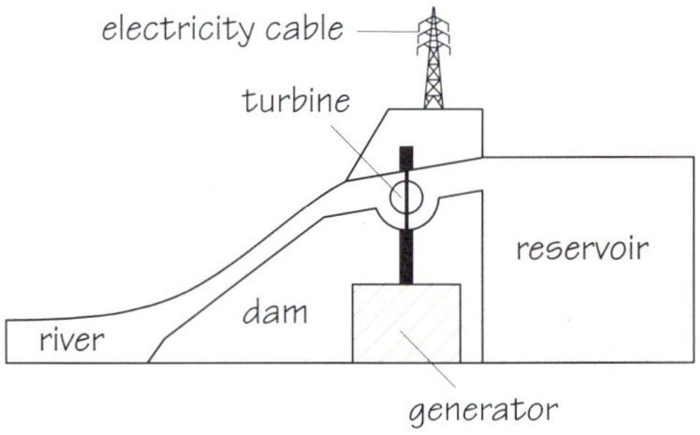

Hydro-electric power is provided by damming a river to form a reservoir → water is released through sluices → water pressure drives turbines → produces electricity
- possible in areas with large rivers
- steep-sided valley of strong impermeable rock is required for a reservoir.

Renewable energy sources have advantages and disadvantages.

Advantages – does not produce any greenhouse gases – once dam is constructed provides cheap electricity – dam prevents flooding – reservoir used for recreation.

Disadvantages – extremely expensive, and difficult, to build – most suitable sites have already been dammed – a large area of land is flooded – reservoirs will slowly silt up.

Wind power

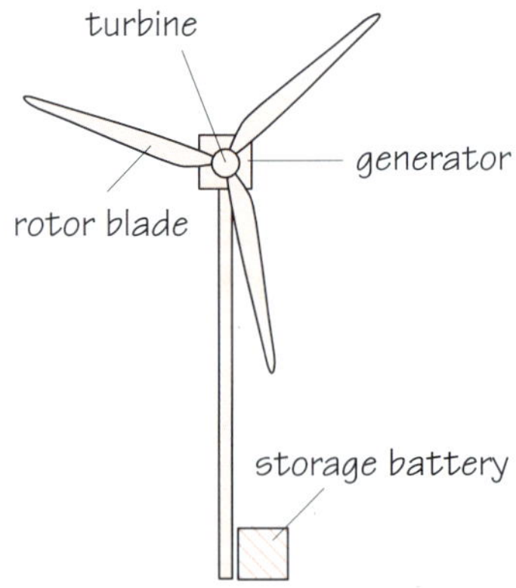

Wind energy – converted into electricity by large **wind turbines**
- the top of the turbine is angled into the wind, which turns the **rotor blades** at up to 400 kph
- wind turbines are most suitable for upland areas with reliable winds.

Advantages – electricity produced is cheap and non-polluting – it is adaptable, e.g. small scale (one turbine for several houses) or large scale (a wind-farm with several hundred turbines).

Disadvantages – visually intrusive, in often beautiful landscapes – would require a huge area to compete with fossil fuels – rotor blades are very noisy for people living nearby.

Solar power

Solar power has greatest potential in LEDCs in the Tropics.

Solar energy is converted into heat and electricity
- hot water is obtained by fixing solar panels to roofs → sunlight heats black panels → water is pumped through panel and then hot water tank → heat transfer takes place
- electricity is obtained using **photo-voltaic cells** made from **silicon** → silicon converts sunlight into electricity
- particularly suitable in areas around the tropics with few clouds.

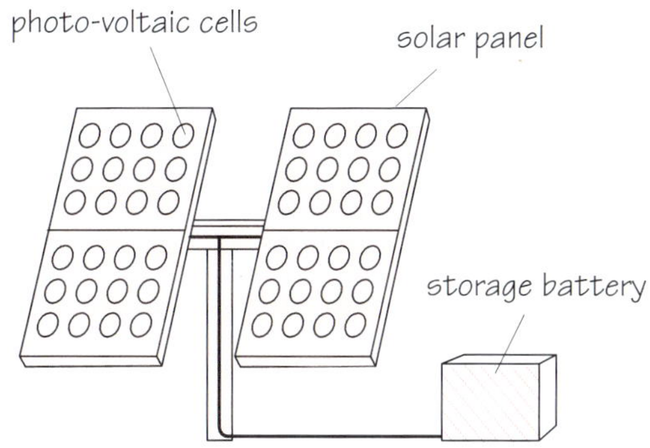

Advantages – a good portable energy source for powering electronic equipment – solar panels on houses save using electricity from national grid.

Disadvantages – limited in use further north and south from equator – does not work at night – photo-voltaic cells are extremely expensive and only convert about 15% of solar energy – would require huge areas of solar panels to provide enough electricity for a city.

Energy conservation

Energy conservation – cutting back on the energy we use and using it in the most efficient way possible
- reduction in consumption is beneficial to environment
- homes can be **insulated** to prevent valuable heat escaping through walls, windows and roofs
- **fluorescent** light bulbs use less electricity
- **cycling** or **public transport** is more efficient than using a car
- smaller cars with more **efficient engines** use less petrol.

Energy

Questions

1 What is the difference between energy and fuel?

2 What is a fossil fuel?

3 What is secondary energy?

4 What is coal formed from?

5 What are its advantages?

6 Why have many UK coal mines closed down?

7 What are oil and gas formed from?

8 As well as fuel, what else is oil used for?

9 Why might we have to 'pay later' for nuclear power?

10 Where is fuelwood a very important energy source?

11 What is meant by the term 'renewable energy'?

12 Reservoirs flood large areas of land. Why does this matter?

13 Why might people not like to live near a wind farm?

14 What type of solar panels are used to make electricity?

15 What does 'energy conservation' mean?

Development and interdependence

Distinguish between the different types of development.

Development – the use of resources and technology to increase wealth and improve standards of living.

- **Economic development** – an increase in income and wealth due to industrial growth.
- **Social development** – an improvement in standard of living through education and healthcare.
- **Environmental development** – improving or restoring the natural environment.
- **Political development** – progression to democracy – free elections.

Development also brings problems.

Inequalities

The terms MEDC, LEDC and Brandt line hide the range of development – many countries are in the middle.

Globally there is a very **unequal distribution** of wealth and standard of living

- MEDCs contain 20% of the world population, yet 80% of the wealth
- MEDCs are mainly in the northern hemisphere – the USA, Europe, Japan – in the southern hemisphere Australia and New Zealand
- LEDCs are mainly in the southern hemisphere – continents of South America, Africa and Asia
- In 1980 the **Brandt Report** identified a dividing line between the world's richer and poorer countries – since then the gap between richest and poorest has continued to grow.

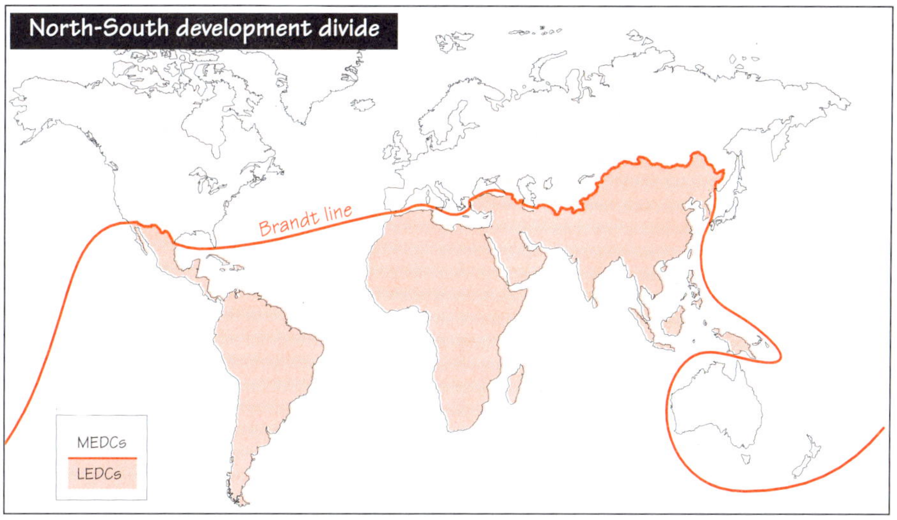

Development indicators

Development indicators – used to give a measure of a country's level of development.

Economic development

GNP is expressed in US dollars so that different countries may be compared.

Economic development is usually measured using **Gross National Product (GNP)**

- GNP is the total value of all goods and services produced by a country in one year, divided by the population to give an average per head.

Social development

Social development may be indicated by population data

- **Birth rate** – number of live births per thousand people per year
- **Death rate** – number of deaths per thousand people per year
- **Infant mortality** – number of infant deaths (less than one year old) per thousand per year
- **Population per doctor** – the number of people to one doctor.

The higher the number of people per doctor → the lower the level of development.

Human Development Index

The **Human Development Index (HDI)** was created by the **United Nations** in 1990
- attempts to combine economic and social development indicators – includes life expectancy, literacy, years of education, and income per person
- recorded as a score from 0 to 1 – 1 being the most developed.

Happiness cannot simply be linked to level of development!

Criticism of development indicators

- GNP on its own ignores social factors
- GNP does not take into account crops grown for subsistence (own use)
- money has different purchasing power in different countries → some countries cheaper
- all indicators are only an average → inequalities exist within countries
- inequality may be found regionally → difference between north and south of a country
- inequality is found in cities → difference between centre and outskirts.

Cycle of underdevelopment

A very important concept.

LEDCs are frequently trapped in a **cycle of underdevelopment**.

In order to develop it is necessary to break the cycle.

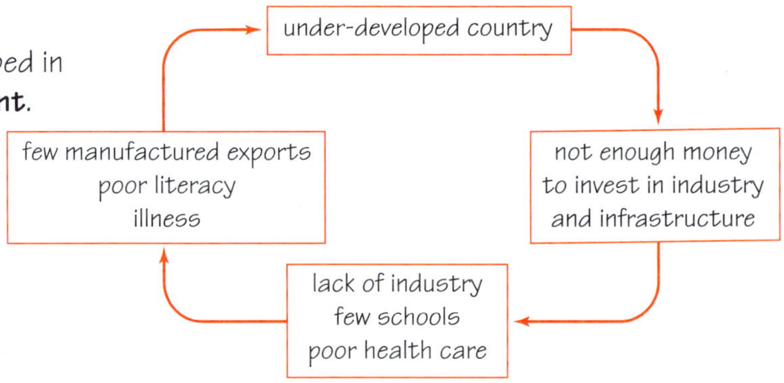

Aspects of underdevelopment

The cycle of underdevelopment can be applied to all these aspects:
- **Population** – LEDCs have rapid population growth → lack of security and high infant mortality drives people to have many children → population increase places greater strain on resources → cancels out any development.
- **Debt** – LEDCs borrowed money from MEDCs → loan interest is up to a third of a countries' earnings → 50 countries cannot afford to meet repayments → limits development of LEDCs.
- **Health** – Lack of health education and medicine results in high death rates → diseases such as malaria and AIDS increasing → depletes workforce → limits development.
- **Housing** – governments cannot provide enough housing → many are homeless or living in squatter settlements → poor living conditions → disease spreads easily.
- **Literacy** – education is expensive → not all go to school → low literacy rate, especially women → unskilled workforce → expertise must be bought from MEDCs.
- **Hazards** – drought, flooding, earthquakes, volcanoes and hurricanes occur → impact is more severe in LEDC than MEDC → buildings are not so strong, rescue services not so well equipped, lack of money for rebuilding → a natural disaster will set back development.
- **Water** – 2 billion people in LEDCs do not have access to clean water → causes disease such as cholera, dysentery and diarrhoea; access to water → hours may be wasted collecting water from wells.
- **Food** – millions do not receive enough food each day → results in undernutrition → tiredness → unable to work; malnutrition occurs when diet is unbalanced → causes health problems.
- **Disease and pests** – disease-spreading insects thrive in hot humid climate of many LEDCs → economic cost with damage to agriculture → social cost to people.

Trade

A country in debt has a **trade deficit.**

Trade – the exchange of goods and services from **producers** to **consumers**
- happens when a country is able to produce goods or services more cheaply, or of better quality, than the consuming country
- a country's **balance of trade** is the difference between money earned from **exports** and money spent on **imports.**

Pattern of trade

General trend is for LEDCs to export primary products (food and raw materials) to MEDCs – MEDCs export manufactured and processed goods to LEDCs
- pattern of trade established since colonial period – 1500 onwards
- Europeans colonised Americas, Africa and Asia → exploited **natural resources** of sugar, cotton, tobacco, spices etc. → imported into Europe
- European countries exported **manufactured goods** to colonised countries, e.g. steam trains to India → gained an economic advantage
- today LEDCs have regained independence – many now export manufactured goods
- poorest countries have not broken original pattern of trade → known as **neo-colonialism**.

Trade barriers

Trade barriers hinder growth and economic development.

These policies are known as **protectionism**.

Governments worried that imports will damage their own industries use **trade barriers**
- **Tariffs** – tax duties are added to cheap imports to make them more expensive.
- **Quotas** – a limit is placed on the number of items that may be imported.
- **Subsidies** – grants are given to home industries to make them more competitive.

Trading groups

GATT (General Agreement on Trade and Tariffs) was agreed between 105 countries in 1993 to increase international trade.

Several groups of countries have formed **free-trade associations**, e.g. the European Union (EU) and the North American Free Trade Association (NAFTA)
- **trading groups** allow tariff and quota free trade between member countries
- common tariff may be used to limit imports from outside the group.

Trade problems for LEDCs

- Value of primary product exports have fallen in value.
- **Dependency** on one or two primary exports is dangerous with fluctuating world prices.
- Exploitation of primary products may damage the environment.
- Primary industry provides fewer jobs than manufacturing.
- LEDCs have limited capital and expertise to invest in manufacturing.
- Manufactured exports from LEDCs have tariffs placed on them by MEDCs.

Fair trade

Fair trade is a policy supported by the **World Trade Organisation** and charities, it includes:
- minimum wages and safe working conditions
- limiting child labour
- environmental protection
- removal of trade barriers
- encouraging retailers to stock 'fair trade' products.

A number of supermarkets now stock fair trade items such as tea and coffee.

Aid

Aid is a transfer of resources from a MEDC to a LEDC; includes money, equipment, food, training, skilled people and loans.

Donors and recipients

– United Nations recommends countries spend 0.7% of **GNP** on aid per year – few do
– largest **donors** in terms of GNP are Norway, Denmark and Sweden
– largest **recipients** are China, Egypt and Indonesia.

The UK donates about 0.3% of GNP as aid.

Types of aid

- **Emergency aid** – short term immediate relief during or after disaster, e.g. famine or hurricane – blankets, tents, medicine, food, clothes, water and equipment are available.
- **Long term aid** – aims to increase development and improve standard of living → may include education and training, technology and improvements to infrastructure.
- **Multilateral aid** – arranged by international organisations – International Monetary Fund (IMF), United Nations (UN) and World Bank.
- **Bilateral aid** – an arrangement between individual governments.
- **Tied aid** – recipient government must agree to spend money on goods from donor country.
- **NGO aid** – Non-Governmental Organisations are charities such as Oxfam who run aid projects – money is raised through private donations and government grants – NGOs are involved with emergency and long-term aid → but not large infrastructure projects.

Advantages and disadvantages of different types of aid is a common exam question.

Advantages of aid

– aid can be beneficial to MEDCs and LEDCs
– tied aid boosts exports and secures jobs in MEDCs, e.g. arms industry
– aid can open markets for goods from MEDCs, e.g. food aid
– aid can improve the standard of living of people living in LEDCs.

Aid rarely reaches the rural areas where the poorest live.

Disadvantages of aid

– LEDCs grow to depend on MEDCs → strengthens **neo-colonial relationship**
– food aid can undercut LEDCs produce → puts farmers out of business
– food aid may alter diets → LEDC becomes more dependent on imports
– tied aid may force LEDCs to buy inappropriate technology, e.g. combine harvesters
– aid is frequently a loan → LEDCs cannot afford repayments
– large scale infrastructure projects damage the environment → increases national debt
– corrupt officials may pocket aid or rich land owners benefit.

Appropriate technology

Appropriate technology development projects are small scale and involve local people
– projects are **low-tech** rather than **hi-tech** → cheaper, and less to go wrong
– local people are in control → less chance of money going astray
– appropriate technology projects do not increase a nation's debt
– schemes may be **labour intensive** → provides employment
– local materials are used → products are cheap
– **local people** are able to afford products.

Appropriate technology schemes are supported by NGOs such as Oxfam.

Development and interdependence

Questions

1 What is economic development?

2 What is meant by 'development indicator'?

3 Why is GNP measured in dollars?

4 What is meant by 'infant mortality rate'?

5 What is the 'HDI' and what does it try to do?

6 Why is 'income' not a good indicator of development?

7 How does poor access to clean water limit development?

8 What is trade?

9 What is meant by 'balance of trade'?

10 What is a quota?

11 What is a 'tariff'?

12 What is the purpose of 'trading groups'?

13 What is 'emergency aid'?

14 Why is 'tied aid' good for MEDCs?

15 What is meant by 'appropriate technology'?

Environmental Geography

Natural environments

People have adapted to the ecosystem that they live in.

Natural environment – the land, water, air and living organisms of the Earth. The natural environment is made up of different **ecosystems**. Ecosystems are increasingly altered by human activity.

Ecosystems

Ecosystem – a community of plants and animals living within a particular environment

- the living organisms, or **biomass**, (plants, animals, bacteria and fungi) are linked to each other and the non-living parts of the ecosystem (rock, soil, water, air and climate)
- range in size from a small patch of moss, to **biomes** such as coniferous forests, extending across continents
- the '**Gaia concept**' considers the Earth as one ecosystem – important when studying global problems such as the ozone layer and global warming.

Succession

At each stage of succession the number and height of plants increases.

Ecosystems take many years to develop through a process called **succession**:

- an area with no vegetation is colonised by simple but tough plants → they are called the **pioneer species**, e.g. lichen
- over time, pioneer species change the conditions to allow larger plants to grow, e.g. grasses
- when the grasses die they rot to form deeper soil → larger plants can now survive, e.g. shrubs
- finally a **dominant species** of tree will be able to take over → succession has been completed
- succession may happen in four environments – **bare rock**, **sand dunes**, **fresh water** and **salt water**
- it is very often interrupted, either by natural events such as floods or volcanic eruptions or by human action such as deforestation, forest fires and agriculture.

In the UK, Oak and Ash trees are dominant.

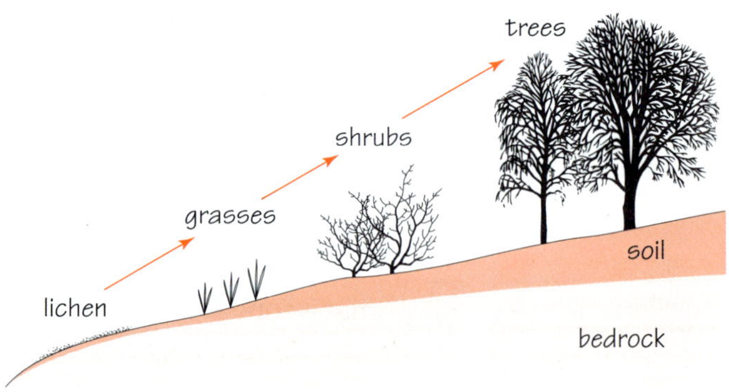

Biomes

Biome – a large ecosystem containing the same type of vegetation

- very closely related to climate → precipitation, temperature, light and wind will control what type of vegetation will grow
- soils will also affect the type of vegetation.

World biomes

When looking at a map of biomes you should remember that it is very generalised and only shows what would be growing there – much of the vegetation has been cut down.

Eight major biomes may be identified:

- Tundra
- Coniferous forest
- Temperate deciduous forest
- Temperate grassland
- Mediterranean
- Desert
- Savanna grassland
- Tropical rainforest.

Three key biomes.

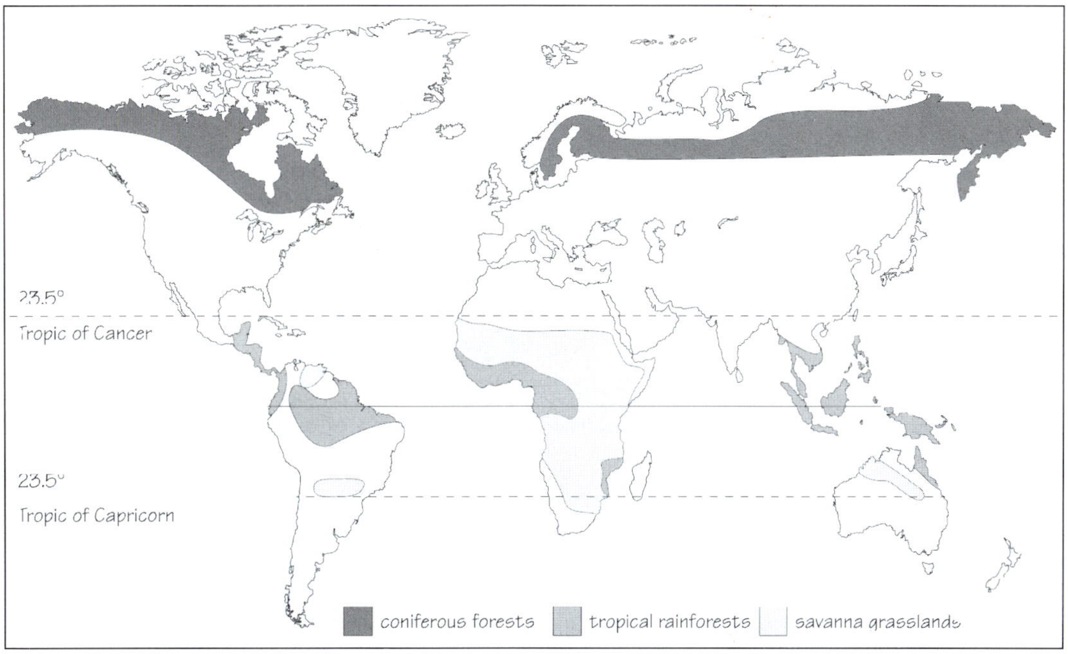

Energy flows

The Sun is the source of all energy in an ecosystem.

Energy flows through an ecosystem in a **food chain**; a series of stages known as **trophic levels**.

Trophic level 1

– **producers**, e.g. grass
– **solar radiation** is converted by plants, through **photosynthesis**, into **carbohydrates**.
– plants are therefore called producers → without plants life could not exist.

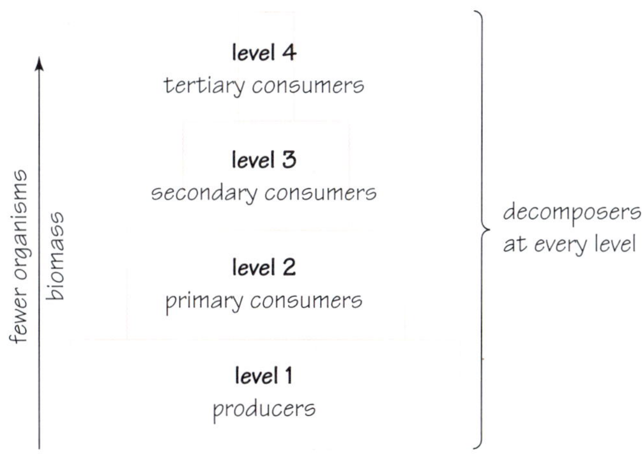

Trophic level 2

– **primary consumers**, e.g. worm
– plants are eaten by animals and insects – **herbivores**
– energy is used for living and is stored as muscle and fat.

Reality is more complicated – animals eat more than one thing → creating a **food web**.

Trophic level 3

– **secondary consumers**, e.g. blackbird
– meat eaters – **carnivores** eat the herbivores
– energy is transferred into the body of the carnivore.

Omnivores eat meat and plants.

Trophic level 4

– **tertiary consumers**, e.g. hawk
– carnivores eat other carnivores → further energy transfer.

If the world's population was vegetarian less food would need to be grown!

- **Decomposers** – bacteria and fungi – exist to break down any **dead organisms** returning energy to the environment as heat.
- **Energy loss** – through **waste** and **heat** – results in a **trophic pyramid** as each trophic level is able to support fewer organisms – biomass.

Nutrient cycle

Cycle occurs quickly in warm and wet ecosystems, e.g. Tropical Rainforests; but very slowly in cold and dry ecosystems, e.g. Tundra.

Nutrients such as **carbon** and **nitrogen** move around an ecosystem in a cycle
– nutrients are released from **weathered** rock into the **soil**
– plants take up the nutrients through their roots
– herbivores eat the plants, and then carnivores eat the herbivores, transferring the nutrients
– plants and animals die → are broken down by decomposers → nutrients are returned to the soil.

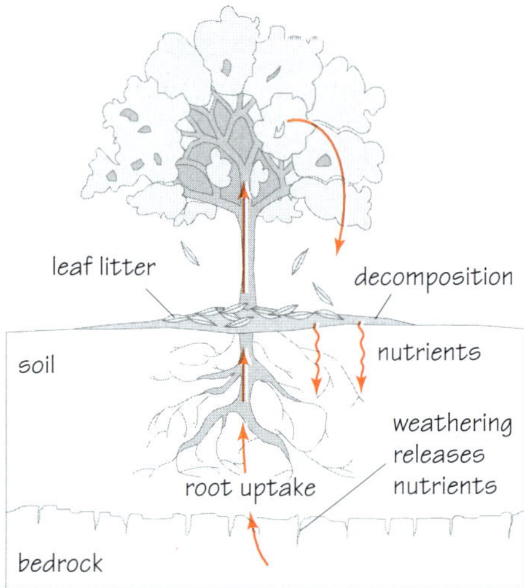

Human modification

People interfere with energy flows and nutrient cycles in ecosystems – not always deliberately.

- The introduction of a **new species** of plant or animal may alter the trophic levels, e.g. introduction of the Cane Toad into Australia → eats any small animal or bird.
- **Agriculture** removes nutrients from the cycle when crops are harvested but also adds nutrients in the form of artificial fertilisers.

Sand dunes

Sand dunes – an example of a small scale ecosystem.
Dunes are formed on the coast when sand blown inland by the wind is trapped by vegetation.

Succession

It is important to understand how vegetation is adapted to its environment.

– **Marram grass** is one of the first species to colonise sand dunes
– marram is adapted to the dry and windy environment → it is able to grow fast so it is not covered by sand → it has long roots to reach water → its leaves fold up and face away from the wind → avoid moisture loss
– inland, behind the main dunes, it is more sheltered → decomposing marram grass has improved the soil → small plants such as **heather** grow.
– further inland taller species such as reeds can survive → followed by small pine trees
– the dominant species will become **Oak** or **Ash trees** once succession is complete.

Threats to sand dunes

- **Recreation** – dunes are popular with tourists → trampling, sliding down dunes, horse riding and fires can damage vegetation → de-stabilises dune which may then 'blow-out'.
- **Water abstraction** – if water table drops plant's roots are unable to reach supply.

- **Military use** – used as a training area for tanks → destroys dunes.
- **Bracken invasion** – becomes dominant, limiting other species.

Sand dune management

Sand dune management interrupts succession to maintain an important ecosystem for plants and animals.

Sand dune erosion is being limited in a number of ways:

- **Education** – signs are erected giving information about the ecosystem.
- **Fencing** – areas are fenced off in rotation to allow recovery.
- **Paths** – mobile wooden boards are laid as pathways to prevent trampling.

Coniferous forests

Location

Coniferous forests are found in a wide band between 50°N and the Arctic Circle – northern Europe to Siberia, USA and Canada.

Climate

- **long winters** with average temperatures –30°C – therefore short growing season
- **low precipitation** → cold dry air unable to hold moisture – summer maximum – total 300 mm
- **short summers** with long days – temperatures around 10°C.

Vegetation and animals

Coniferous forests lack diversity – a single species may dominate.

- **coniferous trees** such as spruce, fir and pine – few other species at ground level due to lack of light and thick layer of pine needles
- conifers are evergreen – keep leaves all year to allow quick photosynthesis
- leaves are needle shaped and waxy – reduces moisture loss (**transpiration**)
- conical tree shape allows snow to slide off – seeds are protected in cones
- few birds – some wolves, bears and beavers.

Soils

- **podsols** – **minerals and humus leached** (washed out) by precipitation → therefore acidic
- thick litter of pine needles → very slow to decompose due to cold climate
- clear **horizons** (layers) due to little mixing → worms do not like acidic soil.

Human activity

- coniferous trees are felled to provide softwood timber and wood pulp for making paper.

Savanna grasslands

Location

Savanna grasslands are located between 25° north and south of the equator in central parts of continents – areas include central Africa and northern Australia.

Climate

- **temperatures are high** throughout the year – an average of 25°C – a short cooler season
- **dry and wet seasons** – wet when sun is overhead → **convectional rainfall** – total 1400 mm
- **dry season** – very little rain – dry winds.

Note how trees and plants adapt to their environment.

Vegetation and animals

- savanna is a transitional area between **tropical rainforest** and **desert**
- **deciduous trees** drop their leaves in the dry season to limit **transpiration**
- trees resist **drought** by having small, waxy, or thorn-like leaves and thick bark
- some trees have fire-resistant trunks and roots long enough to reach the low water table
- grasses grow quickly to a height of up to 5 metres after the rain – die back during dry season
- savanna supports many species of herbivore such as Zebra and Antelope
- several carnivores feed on the herbivores, e.g. Lions.

Soil

- soil is a red coloured **clay** (iron and aluminium oxides)
- **humus** breaks down quickly due to high temperatures but the soil has few nutrients
- a hard layer (**pan**) develops below the surface – makes ploughing and agriculture difficult.

Savanna areas are at risk of desertification.

Human activity

- savanna is most suitable for **nomadic pastoralism** → grazing animals such as cattle or sheep
- crops can be grown, including tobacco, maize and millet.

Tropical rainforests

Location

Tropical rainforests are located 5° north and south of the equator, areas include Indonesia and Brazil.

Climate

- **high temperatures** all year – average 27°C – twelve hours of daylight each day
- **high humidity** resulting in **convectional rainfall** every afternoon – over 2000 mm a year.

Vegetation and animals

- the most **diverse biome** with over 300 species of tree per km^2, e.g. teak and mahogany
- trees are deciduous – shed leaves all year
- clear layers of vegetation can be identified – tallest trees called **emergents** – up to 50 metres
- top layer – **canopy**, over 30 metres high – most insects, birds and animals live at this level
- second layer – **undercanopy**, up to 20 metres
- third layer – **shrub layer**, up to 10 metres – shrubs and small trees
- trees have **buttress roots** to support great height and '**drip tips**' on leaves to shed rainfall
- undergrowth is limited due to little light penetrating at ground level
- many thousands of species of wildlife.

Soil

- red **clay** soils – up to 30 metres deep – rapid breakdown of leaf litter due to humid climate
- soils are **infertile** → **leaching** occurs due to high rainfall
- most **nutrients** are stored in the **biomass**.

One hectare of rainforest may contain up to 5000 trees.

Deforestation

Deforestation of tropical rainforests has become an issue of global concern – it is believed that they contain up to 90% of all of the species of plants and animals on Earth – in the last 50 years over half of the world's rainforests have been cut down.

Rainforests are found mainly in LEDCs, which are under pressure to develop.

Causes

- **Population growth** – land is needed for farming and housing.
- **Roads** – new roads have allowed access to areas of forest previously very difficult to reach.
- **Timber** – hardwoods are exported, usually to richer countries.
- **Mining** – areas deforested for open cast mining of resources, e.g. iron and aluminium ore.
- **Cattle ranching** – forests cleared to provide grassland for cattle (beef exported).
- **Foreign debt** – money earned from timber and ore exports is used to pay back loans from richer countries.
- **HEP** – reservoirs created by hydro-electric power schemes flood large areas of forest.

Benefits

– jobs are provided in logging and mining industries
– money from exports may be used to improve quality of life, e.g. schools and hospitals.

Problems

- Nutrients in rainforest ecosystem are stored in **biomass** → if biomass is removed an infertile soil is left → results in crop failure for new farmers after only three or four harvests.
- Soil erosion occurs due to heavy rainfall on exposed soil → leads to **desertification** → soil will silt up rivers → damages water supply – navigation problems for boats.
- Global climate change may occur – rainforests absorb CO_2 → deforestation will increase concentration of CO_2 in atmosphere → one cause of **global warming**.
- Medicines for diseases such as malaria have been discovered in rainforest plants – every week plants that have not been studied become extinct → new cures may be lost.
- Indigenous forest people are losing homes and culture – diseases have been introduced by settlers.

A common exam question.

Conflicts

- MEDC governments put pressure on LEDCs to stop deforestation → blame them for increasing global warming → however MEDCs are largest importers of timber.
- LEDC governments need profit from exports for development – point out MEDCs have already deforested their own countries – MEDCs also burn 80% of world's fossil fuels – main cause of global warming.
- Loggers and indigenous peoples may be involved in violent conflicts during deforestation.
- Environmental groups such as 'Friends of the Earth' campaign to raise awareness of problem – put pressure on governments of both importers and exporters.

Solutions

Manage forests in a sustainable way – calculate how much timber grows each year → remove only this new growth.

MEDCs must be prepared to share the cost of conserving the rainforests.

- **Selective felling** of valuable mature trees only → prevent clear felling.
- Transport harvested logs by helicopter → roads not necessary.
- Harvest valuable products such as Brazil nuts → provides long term income.
- People living in MEDCs should buy only timber approved by the Forest Stewardship Council (FSC) → ensures only sustainable logging.

Natural environments

Questions

1 What is an ecosystem?

2 What is succession?

3 What is a biome?

4 Where does the energy in an ecosystem come from?

5 What is meant by 'producer'?

6 What trophic level is a tertiary consumer?

7 What is the main source of nutrients in an ecosystem?

8 How does climate affect the nutrient cycle?

9 What type of vegetation is a pioneer species on sand dunes?

10 How are coniferous trees' leaves adapted to their environment?

11 What type of vegetation is found in a savanna biome?

12 Where are tropical rainforests found?

13 Where are most of the nutrients in a rainforest biome stored?

14 Why do HEP schemes damage forests?

15 Why does deforestation only result in short term profit?

Global environmental concerns

Most exams contain a question on these global environmental problems.

Development brings environmental problems at different scales → some problems can be dealt with on a local or national scale → other **environmental concerns** have no borders.

Ozone layer depletion – global warming – acid deposition – all need to be tackled on a global basis.

Ozone layer depletion

Ozone layer depletion is the thinning of a layer of protective gas around the Earth.

Ozone (O_3) – a gas that at ground level is harmful to humans
- found in a layer of the atmosphere 25 to 30 km above the Earth
- absorbs and filters **Ultra-Violet (UV)** radiation from the Sun
- UV radiation causes skin to tan and in small doses is good for you → produces **vitamin D**.

Damage to the ozone layer

Many people confuse global warming, acid rain and ozone layer depletion.

Chlorofluorocarbons (CFCs) – are man-made chemicals
- used in aerosols, foam packaging and as coolant for fridges and air-conditioning
- are light gases which slowly rise into the atmosphere – some have a life of 400 years
- CFCs attack and destroy Ozone – one CFC molecule can destroy 100 000 ozone molecules.

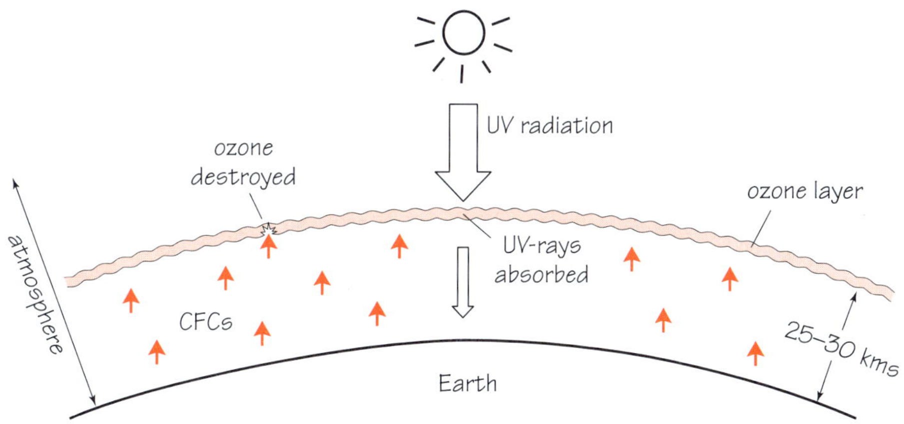

Consequences

In the 1980s holes in the ozone layer were discovered above the Arctic and Antarctic
- the ozone layer was also significantly thinner over countries such as Australia and Chile
- UV radiation is not being filtered
- **skin cancer** has increased

A 1% depletion of ozone = 5% increase in skin cancer.

– **eye cataracts** are now more common
– **crops are damaged** → increases disease and reduces yield
– **marine life affected** – UV radiation can penetrate sea to 20 metres depth → may alter ecosystem.

Solutions

- **International agreement was reached in 1987 to ban use of CFCs by 2000.**
- Most MEDCs have already achieved target – LEDCs need extension.
- Fridges, freezers and air conditioning units can be dismantled to remove CFCs.
- Aerosols are now labelled as 'ozone friendly'.
- Biodegradable packaging is often used instead of foam.
- **Burn times** are now given with weather forecast in summer in UK.
- Public awareness has increased due to the media – sun-tan lotion sales are up!

Global warming

Note the difference between the greenhouse effect and global warming.

Global warming is caused by the **greenhouse effect.**

Greenhouse effect

The **greenhouse effect** is the way the Earth is able to trap heat within its atmosphere:
– **Solar energy** from the Sun reaches Earth as **shortwave radiation**
– Earth's surface **re-radiates** energy as **longwave radiation**
– atmospheric gases including **water vapour**, **carbon dioxide (CO_2)** and **methane (CH_4)** are able to absorb longwave radiation
– therefore atmosphere retains heat – if the greenhouse effect did not exist the Earth would be a frozen wasteland
– however, the greenhouse effect appears to be increasing as the Earth is becoming warmer – **global warming**.

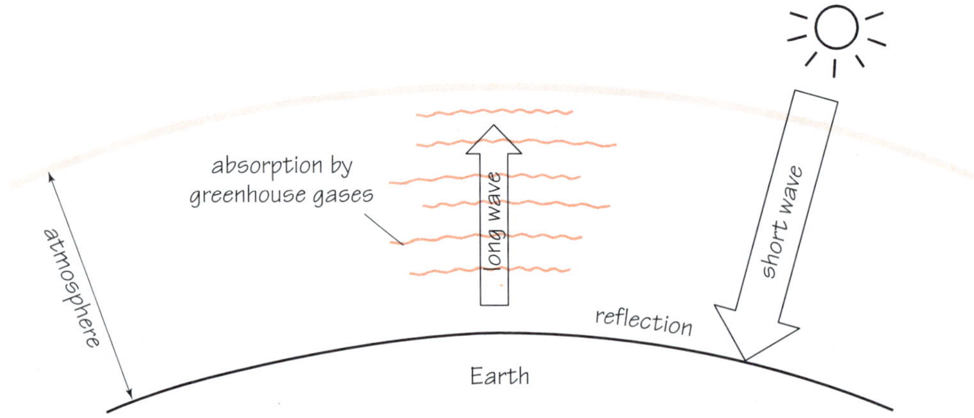

Causes

- **Fossil fuels** – **carbon dioxide** is released into the atmosphere when fossil fuels are burned.
  Since the Industrial Revolution (late 18th century) the rate at which fossil fuels are burned has increased → used to provide energy for industry, homes and transport.
- **Deforestation** – trees convert CO_2 into oxygen.

Majority of temperate forests already felled → tropical forests now being cut down
- **Ranching** – growth in cattle farming for beef and milk.
  Cattle produce **methane** in intestine → increase in methane
  = increase in greenhouse effect.

Global warming would benefit some areas.

Consequences

Consequences of global warming would be environmental, economic and social.

- predicted increase in global temperatures of between 1°C and 4°C by 2040
- **polar ice caps** will melt → sea level will rise by up to 1.5 metres → low lying areas in countries such as Bangladesh and Holland will be flooded → millions of refugees
- climate and vegetation patterns will move → deserts will spread
- an increase in extreme weather such as **droughts** and **hurricanes**
- an increase in diseases such as malaria as places become warmer and more humid.

Slowing global warming

- Reduce emissions of greenhouse gases – Earth Summit in Rio de Janeiro (1992), 118 countries agreed **Agenda 21** → a plan to reduce pollution on a local scale.
- Earth Summit in Kyoto (1997) – limited success so far → USA refused to limit emissions.
- Deforestation – stop clear felling → encourage **selective felling** which allows re-growth.
- Increase tree planting programmes.
- Reduce population growth → fewer energy resources used up.

Evidence against global warming

Some scientists do not agree that global warming is being caused by people.
- Earth's climate has always fluctuated between ice ages and hotter periods.
- **Water vapour** is far more important as a greenhouse gas than CO_2 → therefore increase in CO_2 will make no difference.

Acid deposition

Acid deposition is the correct term since it may be dry or wet.

Acid deposition is fall-out from the atmosphere of acidic compounds – either in rain, as **acid rain** – or in very small particles, as **dry deposition**.

Acid rain was first noticed in Scandinavia in the 1950s → it has become a problem for several industrialised nations, particularly the USA, Canada, Sweden and Norway.

Acidity

- **pH** is a measure of **acidity** or **alkalinity** – scale is from 0 (acid) to 14 (alkali) – a **neutral** liquid will have a pH of 7
- precipitation is naturally acidic – CO_2 mixes with rainwater to form **carbonic acid** – pH 5 to 6.
- acid rain caused by pollution has a pH of 4 to 4.5.

Causes

- Power stations and oil refineries release **sulphur dioxide (SO_2)** and **nitrogen oxide (NO)**.
- Vehicles release nitrogen oxide.

- Acidic compounds SO_2 and NO are carried by wind.
- Dry deposition of compounds as a gas occurs within 250 km of source.
- **Sulphur dioxide** combines with rainfall to form **sulphuric acid**.
- **Nitrogen oxide** combines with rainfall to form **nitric acid**.
- Wet deposition as 'acid rain' occurs up to 2000 km from source → therefore the polluting country may not suffer the effects.

Consequences

– acid rain **leaches nutrients** from soil → **damages forests**
– coniferous forests are dying → acid attacks needles → turn yellow and drop
– trees more at greater risk from disease and insect attack
– lake water increases in acidity → plant life, fish and amphibians die
– water supply is contaminated → acidic water damages copper pipes
– acidity in soil restricts crop growth → yields are decreasing
– limestone and marble buildings are being **weathered** more rapidly → attacked by **chemical weathering**, e.g. Taj Mahal in India.

Reducing acid deposition

International co-operation is needed to reduce the problem of acid deposition.

- Dry deposition can be reduced by increasing height of chimneys → pollutants will be carried further away → wet deposition becomes worse.
- Filters may be fitted to power station chimneys to remove SO_2 and NO from emissions → would increase electricity bills by 10%.
- Lime (alkali) may be added to lakes to restore pH → only a temporary solution.
- In 1988 an EU directive required SO_2 emissions to be reduced 40% by 1998 → has happened due to switch to gas, away from coal.

Issues

Some people argue that the acidity is caused by the coniferous trees themselves.

Acid deposition causes disagreement between countries.

- Sweden blames the UK for poisoning its forests and lakes → prevailing south-west wind carries our pollution north-east to Scandinavia.
- Canada blames the USA for allowing its pollution to cross the border and damage its ecosystems.

Sustainable development

Learn this definition – it can be applied to many topics.

Sustainable development meets the needs of the present without compromising the ability of future generations to meet their needs.

- Development is the aim of all countries → to increase wealth and living standards.
- Increases in development result in more natural resources being used → eventually some will run out.
- Resources are being used for short-term gains while ignoring the long term costs.
- Profits from resource exploitation should be invested now to find an alternative for when that resource runs out.
- **Reducing consumption** and **re-cycling** our resources should be a priority – especially in MEDCs.

Global environmental concerns

Questions

1 How is ozone beneficial to life on earth?

2 What chemicals damage ozone?

3 What can be done to reduce ozone layer damage?

4 What is global warming?

5 What is the greenhouse effect?

6 What type of radiation is reflected from the Earth's surface?

7 What are the most important greenhouse gases?

8 Why does deforestation make global warming worse?

9 What is Agenda 21?

10 How might a reduction in population growth slow global warming?

11 What is the difference between acid rain and dry deposition?

12 Which two gases are most responsible for acid deposition?

13 How does acid rain affect trees?

14 How does acid deposition affect buildings?

15 Why does acid rain lead to disagreements between countries?

Answers

Physical Geography

Earthquakes and volcanoes

1 Continental (sial), Oceanic (sima) **2** Convection currents in the mantle **3** Two oceanic plates moving apart **4** Land buckles when two plates converge **5** Destructive **6** Conservative **7** Layers of ash and lava **8** A mudflow **9** Ash in atmosphere reflects sunlight **10** Surface point directly above focus **11** Ground behaves as a liquid **12** Seismograph **13** Earthquake damage **14** Buildings not earthquake proof, fewer resources to deal with after effects **15** Ash and lava weather to form fertile soil

Rocks, resources and landscapes

1 Igneous **2** Rocks changed by extreme heat or pressure **3** Metamorphic **4** Shells of tiny prehistoric sea creatures **5** Bedding plane **6** Pervious **7** Weathering caused by heating and cooling (exfoliation) **8** Scree **9** Shape of the land **10** Shrinking when cooling **11** Tors **12** Steep slope on chalk upland (downs) **13** Water supply is limited **14** Joints are weathered and eroded **15** Governments need money in order to develop and to pay debts

Rivers and water management

1 Continuous circling of water between the sea, atmosphere and land **2** Trees, plants and buildings **3** When rainfall is unable to infiltrate into the ground – soil may be saturated **4** Downward movement of water through soil into permeable rock **5** The area of land drained by a river and its tributaries **6** A watershed **7** Hydraulic action, corrasion/abrasion, attrition, corrosion **8** When it loses energy **9** Erosion and deposition **10** Material deposited by a river **11** A low lying area of land extending into the sea or a lake at a river mouth **12** Relationship between precipitation and discharge **13** Steep slopes, impermeable rock, sparse vegetation and a small drainage basin **14** Impermeable surfaces of concrete and tarmac, and drains, increase the speed and amount of surface run-off **15** By preventing new building in areas at risk from flooding

Coasts

1 Wind blowing over surface of the sea **2** When it reaches shallow water **3** Fetch **4** Limestone and chalk **5** Longshore drift **6** Where there are alternating bands of hard and soft rock – soft rock is eroded more quickly **7** Stack **8** Gently sloping area of rock at the foot of a sea cliff **9** Granite **10** River mouth or where the coast changes direction **11** Salt marsh **12** Water is stored in glaciers and ice sheets **13** A fiord is a flooded glacial valley, a ria is a flooded river valley **14** Beach material wired together as a coastal defence **15** By depriving other areas of beach material

Glaciation

1 A mass of ice formed in a mountain valley **2** Snow compressed to form ice **3** Ten thousand years ago **4** They are able to bend **5** Removal of rocks by a glacier **6** The glacier has less erosive power here **7** Arête **8** U-shaped **9** Occur where hanging valleys are present **10** Interlocking spurs which have had ends eroded to form steep cliffs **11** Melting **12** Egg shaped hills formed from glacial till **13** Sorted by glacial meltwater **14** Valleys are wide, deep and sparsely populated **15** Waterfalls harnessed for HEP

Weather and climate

1 Weather describes atmospheric conditions at a certain time and place, climate is the average weather of a place over many years **2** High pressure **3** Differences in air pressure **4** A warm air mass and cold air mass meeting **5** Actual amount of water vapour present in the atmosphere expressed as a percentage of the maximum which could be held **6** High pressure air mass **7** Rising **8** Warm air mass lifted off ground by

cold air mass **9** Isobars **10** Minus 6°C **11** Warmed by North Atlantic Drift and warm south-west winds **12** It is in the rain shadow – rain has fallen in the west **13** Between 5° north and south of the equator **14** Lack of cloud cover allows heat to escape **15** Sea temperatures over 27°C

Human Geography

Population and migration

1 How people are spread out over an area **2** Does not show local variations or gradual changes **3** Population doubles every generation **4** To allow comparisons between countries **5** Death rates exceed birth rates and population is falling **6** They can afford to import resources from LEDCs **7** Women gain more control over whether they have children **8** The make up of a population in terms of age, sex and life expectancy **9** Males have migrated, or been killed in a war **10** Workers – between 15 and 65 years old **11** Migration from countryside to city **12** Increase in the percentage of people living in cities **13** Movement from cities to the countryside **14** Blamed for taking jobs and housing **15** A person forced to leave an area

Settlement and urbanisation

1 Site is the exact location of a settlement, situation is the location of the settlement in relation to the surrounding area **2** Social and economic activities of a settlement **3** Conurbation **4** Maximum distance people are prepared to travel to use a service **5** Goods purchased infrequently – compare prices **6** Supermarket **7** Urbanisation is an increase in the percentage of people living in cities, urban growth is the expansion of towns and cities **8** Industrial Revolution **9** Decline of housing and service quality **10** Redevelopment involves large scale demolition, rehabilitation aims to improve existing buildings **11** Low quality housing bought and improved **12** Migration from urban to rural areas **13** To contain urban sprawl and provide recreation **14** Squatter settlements are unplanned therefore lack basic services – located on outskirts, miles from CBD **15** Lack of fresh water, sewerage, waste removal and health services

Agriculture

1 Inputs = soil, climate   Processes = weeding, grazing   Outputs = Crops, profit **2** Number of days temperature is above 6°C **3** Temperatures decrease by 6°C every 1000 metres of altitude, more exposed to wind and rain **4** Nutrients are released from weathered bedrock, impermeable bedrock may cause waterlogging, permeable bedrock results in little surface drainage **5** Government limit on maximum production **6** Subsistence produces food for farmer and family, commercial aims to make profit **7** Common Agricultural Policy **8** EU guaranteed minimum price for agricultural produce **9** Access for larger farm machinery **10** A move away from traditional farming into other related areas of business **11** Increase in agricultural output caused by introduction of hi-tech farming methods in LEDCs **12** Artificial watering of crops **13** Wealthy land owners **14** Seeds must be purchased every year, require specific fertilisers and pesticides **15** Surpluses are exported, poor cannot afford to buy it

Industry

1 Primary, secondary, tertiary, quaternary **2** Percentage of workers involved in primary, secondary and tertiary industry **3** Types of jobs change as a country industrialises **4** Change from manufacturing to service industries **5** Electricity is supplied by cable **6** Industries remain concentrated in an area although the factors responsible for their original location are no longer important **7** Raw materials **8** Not tied to raw material or market **9** Reduced taxes and planning laws for ten years **10** Difference between money earned from exports and money spent on imports by a country **11** Transnational Corporation **12** Transport networks poor, often affected by weather, unreliable telephone systems **13** Newly Industrialised Country **14** When tax holiday ends, companies relocate **15** Return warm water with low oxygen content to river

Leisure and tourism

1 Activities undertaken during leisure time, lasting less than 24 hours **2** Paid holiday, shorter working week, higher wages **3** Earlier retirement and increased life expectancy **4** Flights, accommodation and food included in price **5** Areas outside Europe **6** Provides income for a country **7** Tourism is affected by different times of the year **8** Seasonal unemployment **9** Large area of attractive countryside protected by law **10** Ten **11** Provided employment **12** Area that attracts most tourists **13** Develop other sites **14** Investment in airports, road, hotels and advertising **15** Avoid mass tourism, encourage small groups of wealthy tourists, protect the environment

Energy

1 Energy is power, fuel is a store of energy **2** Fuel formed millions of years ago **3** Fuel converted into electricity **4** Fossilised trees and plants **5** Large reserves, efficient **6** Competition from oil, gas and cheaper imported coal **7** Fossilised remains of tiny sea creatures **8** Products such as petrol and plastic **9** Decommissioning of nuclear power stations is very expensive, radioactive waste takes hundreds of years to become safe **10** LEDCs **11** Inexhaustible energy, can be used for ever **12** Agricultural land is lost, people may lose homes **13** Visual and noise pollution **14** Photo-voltaic cells **15** Reducing amount of energy used

Development and interdependence

1 Increase in income and wealth, industrial growth **2** A measure of development **3** To enable comparisons between countries **4** Number of infant deaths per thousand per year **5** Human Development Index combines economic and social development indicators **6** Money has different purchasing power in different countries **7** Causes disease, time wasted in collection **8** Exchange of goods and services **9** Difference between money earned from exports and spent on imports **10** Limit on number of imports **11** Tax added to imported goods **12** To allow free-trade between member countries **13** Short term emergency relief **14** Boosts exports and secures jobs **15** Small scale, low tech, involve local people

Environmental Geography

Natural environments

1 Community of plants and animals living in a particular environment **2** The colonisation and development of vegetation **3** Large ecosystem containing the same type of vegetation **4** Sun **5** Plants converting solar energy into carbohydrates **6** Level 4 **7** Weathered bedrock **8** Quick in warm, wet areas, slow in cold dry areas **9** Marram grass **10** Needle shaped and waxy to reduce transpiration **11** Deciduous drought resistant trees and grasses **12** 5° north and south of equator **13** Biomass **14** Large areas of forest flooded **15** Trees will not grow back, soil fertility declines rapidly

Global environmental concerns

1 Filters UV radiation **2** Chlorofluorocarbons (CFCs) **3** Ban CFC's **4** Increase in temperature of the Earth **5** Absorption of solar energy by atmospheric gases **6** Longwave **7** Water vapour, carbon dioxide, methane **8** Trees convert carbon dioxide into oxygen **9** Reducing pollution on a local scale **10** Fewer energy resources would be needed **11** Acidic compounds deposited in rain or as a gas **12** Sulphur dioxide, nitrogen oxide **13** Attacks leaves and needles **14** Increases rate of chemical weathering **15** Country affected may not be the polluter